Research for Europe

A resources toolbox for Ontario exporters

Maggie Weaver

2018 edition

IGUANA

Publisher: Mary Ann J. Blair
Cover design: Ruth Dwight
Interior design: Meghan Behse

ISBN (paperback): 978-1-77180-243-7
ISBN (EPUB): 978-1-77180-245-1
ISBN (Kindle): 978-1-77180-246-8

This is an original print edition of *Research for Europe*.

Contents

1. The market research process

1a. Research objectives

It may seem that your goal is simply to find out as much as you can about the market. But the ultimate purpose of market research is to uncover insights that will help you validate assumptions or make strategic decisions.

For example, the primary objective of the research may be to decide between two geographic markets: Will my first target market in Europe be the UK, or will I start with Belgium as a test market for later expansion into France and Germany? Or the primary objective may be to determine if your bestselling product in Canada will be the first product line you introduce into Europe.

In practice, market research is an iterative process – insights from your first effort will lead you to explore further, and you can then undertake a second research project with a more focused, or even tangential, objective.

Your specific approach to market research will depend on the outcome that you want.

1b. Research design

Research design refers to your approach: a roadmap of your research steps, based on your objective.

For example, if you're comparing two possible geographic markets for a consumer product, you might start by finding socio-demographic statistics in those countries, or data on the number and size of the appropriate retail outlets – using sources listed in Section 3e Statistics. If you have an industrial product or service, you might start by looking for an overview of the target industry in each country – in Section 6 Sectors.

The design roadmap for the first iteration of the research may be broad, as you check out interesting by-ways, whereas the design roadmap for the subsequent iterations may specify particular resources to be explored in depth.

So the research design – the sequence of your search for specific information and the type of sources that you'll use – will vary with the research objective.

1c. The export plan

As you follow your roadmap and execute your research design, record your journey; organize the data and your insights into an export plan. Examples of export plans are in the resources described in Section 2 Export guides. As you probably do with your vacation mementos, be sure to annotate each piece of information with its source (association, URL, trade advisor, statistics agency, etc.).

Just as the vacation mementos may be thematic rather than chronological, the order that the information finally appears in your export plan may not match your research steps – the design. In fact, sometimes an insight is important enough to appear several times in the plan.

Most of the information you find will be about potential markets and how to reach customers there (i.e., marketing); it will be logged into the "market overview" and "market entry plan" sections of your export plan.

You'll also find ideas for other parts of the plan – for example, region or country overviews may highlight risk factors that will need to be addressed; network contacts in bi-lateral associations may uncover potential in-market strategic partners; regulatory sources may alert you to the importance of retaining tax or intellectual property professionals.

Having an export plan is often a condition for receiving government funding. Section 10 Checklist... indicates which toolbox sections will be useful for completing the various parts of your own export plan.

1d. Primary and secondary research

Much of the market information needed for your export plan is already out there, available from government agencies, industry journal publishers, and competitor websites – all "external" sources. "Internal" sources will also yield insights; for example, statistics about your website's visitors will indicate their country of origin and the web pages which interest them. Pulling information from these external and internal secondary sources is called secondary research or desk research.

Primary research, on the other hand, means finding data and insights specifically for this research project – information that was not previously available in one spot. For example, you may need to visit the target market to compare the prices that competitors are charging for similar products, or you may need a focus group of target users to test the translated installation guide that will accompany your equipment. Primary research involves surveys, focus groups, visits to the target market and other expensive activities.

A sensible approach is to do secondary research first, aiming for quality rather than quantity. Then design a new research project to fill the most important gaps in your knowledge using further secondary or primary research.

This toolbox covers *external secondary sources*.

1e. Customer and market types

Market research firms distinguish between consumer market research and B2B (business to business) research.

In consumer markets, the number of potential buyers may be very large, with small groups of consumers (segments) having different preferences, perceptions and motivations. Consumer buying behaviour also varies between frequent purchases such as food and infrequent purchases such as financial services and durables. For your export plan, collect basic demographic data and information on competing products or services, but also research market entry partners such as retailers who can provide insights into complexities like local appeal.

B2B products and services have typically far fewer potential customers, who are more easily identified since they are companies, institutions or government agencies. But the purchasing process within each organization involves influencers, such as a technical department which sets specifications, a financial department which imposes budgets, and the purchasing department which places the order. Again, collect basic information about the buying organization, and also research sales agents and similar specialists who have insights into target customer organizations.

Trade advisors also distinguish between fast-paced economies and relationship-based economies. In fast-paced economies such as North America and Western Europe, quality and service excellence dominate, especially for B2B. In relationship-based economies, such as southern Europe, established suppliers are stiff competition and exporters must take time to develop a relationship with the potential customer. Consumer purchasing is also increasingly relationship based, with strong brand loyalty for even commodity-type products.

For these reasons, researching your market entry options is as important as researching potential buyers.

1f. Exportable services

In recent years, Canada's fastest growing exports have included financial and insurance services, management services, and IT services. In addition to such services that are delivered directly to foreign customers, exported *products* can include services such as R&D and maintenance that contribute as much as one-third of their market value.

Because services are intangible, marketing them to foreign buyers is harder than marketing goods; market entry involves different types of partners, business viability indicators are different, and market research is often more complex. And there are often visa, tax and intellectual property issues when delivering the service.

Perhaps reflecting these difficulties, there are few guides specific to exporting services, and few statistics sources. However, the recently completed Canada-EU Comprehensive Economic & Trade Agreement (CETA) has an important services component, and Canada is a party in negotiations for an international Trade in Services Agreement (TISA), so more information and support may be forthcoming.

In this toolbox, services resources appear mostly in Section 6 Sectors: professional services (e.g., legal and financial), construction (e.g., architecture and engineering), clean technology (environmental services) and information & communications (ICT).

1g. Next steps

As you add information and insights to your draft export plan, two "next steps" will become apparent.

In the more complete sections of the export plan you'll be able to come to some conclusions or decisions as to your best target markets, necessary product or service adjustments, market entry approach, and areas where you'll need specialist help such as tax or legal advice. There'll also be sections where you don't have enough data to inform your decisions (for example, pricing strategy).

So, do some more focused research to identify the specialists and to fill those knowledge gaps.

But then take your export plan, gaps and all, to a trade advisor at Global Affairs Canada (see *http://tradecommissioner.gc.ca/ontario/index.aspx*), the Ontario Ministry of International Trade (see *https://www.ontario.ca/page/ministry-international-trade*) or Ontario Ministry of Agriculture, Food and Rural Affairs (*http://www.omafra.gov.on.ca/english/food/export/index.html*) if you are a food company. These experts will provide further insights into your target market, assess your company's export readiness, and introduce you to valuable programs and services that will support you as you take your business to Europe.

And now, let's get researching!

ILLUSTRATION: Mike wonders how his engineering consulting firm might benefit from the Canada-EU CETA. In North America, his company bids directly and with partners on water and wastewater projects.

Step 1: The guides in **Section 2a** highlight the improved access CETA offers to government procurement at regional & municipal levels, and in public utilities. In **Section 6** two sectors are of interest: government procurement (i.e., his customers) and clean technology (his own sector). From these, Mike browses a guide to public procurement under CETA, and a US government Environmental Technologies Resource Guide. This latter describes the EU's Urban Waste Water Treatment Directive (UWWTD), discloses the fact that related EU spending is in countries in eastern Europe, and references the UK as having a lot of work to do in this area.

Step2: Do more **focused research** on the UK market and potential market entry partners. Back to Section 6 – in Contracts Finder for the UK, Mike studies previously awarded contracts for names of potential local partners, and EU's List of Cluster Organizations, and finds the Water Cluster based in East Anglia and some local engineering firms listed on the cluster's website.

Step 3: Mike's **next steps** involve three main activities. He will follow up on the programs and funding described in Section 6, particularly the WaterTAP program in Ontario. He will also find out if his current North American partners can help him in Europe, especially the UK (an example of *internal* secondary research). And, as a longer-term option, he will check the European Environment Agency website at *https://www.eea.europa.eu* for data and publications related to UWWTD projects and funds.

2. Export guides

When we learn to cook, we learn to read the recipe first to see the whole process from start to finish. The resources in this section describe the recipe for exporting; they alert you to the government programs and services for exporters which, along with your own market research, are key ingredients. The guides often contain checklists and export plan outlines; another export plan outline is in Section 10.

There are also guides specific to exporting to Europe, and to European countries, often written from the viewpoint of the import country. So in addition to providing general guidance, these more focused guides can offer ideas for further lines of enquiry, as they describe the intricacies of the import processes in more detail, and the contacts provided will be more pertinent. See also Section 6 for *sector*-specific guides.

2a. General export guides

Introduction to Exporting – How to Sell to International Markets
http://www.edc.ca/EN/Knowledge-Centre/Publications/Pages/default.aspx

Export Development Canada. Chapters include establishing your presence abroad, dealing with international contracts, getting paid, financing your exports, trade compliance and trade barriers, logistics and delivery, the legal dimension, and maintaining the relationship. 75 pages, 2012. (Registration required.)

Step-by-Step Guide to Exporting
http://tradecommissioner.gc.ca/exporters-exportateurs/guide-exporting-guide-exportation.aspx

Trade Commissioner Service. Contents include getting started, assessing your company's export readiness, developing an export plan, identifying your target market, developing your export marketing strategy, entering the target market, identifying shippers and shipping, planning your export financing, the legal side of international trade, and e-business for exporters. 91 pages. (Registration required.)

Getting Ready to Export Guide
https://www.ontario.ca/document/getting-ready-export

Ontario Ministry of International Trade. Written for businesses new to exporting. Covers how to determine if your company is ready to export, how to develop an export plan and how to make international contacts. The appendix includes contacts and resources, and some sample forms required to export. 52 pages, 2016.

A Basic Guide to Exporting
https://www.export.gov/export-education

US Trade Information Center. Written for US small businesses. Separate articles will be useful for Canadian companies: developing a strategy; developing a marketing plan; methods and channels; finding qualified buyers; exporting services; international legal considerations; e-exporting tools for small businesses; shipping your product; pricing, quotations and terms; methods of payment; business travel abroad; and selling overseas and after-sales service.

Export Business Planner
https://www.sba.gov/sites/default/files/SBA%20Export%20Bu siness%20Planner.pdf

> US Small Business Administration. Written for US small businesses. Each chapter has two primary content areas: informational pages and customizable worksheets that enable the user to work through the process. It includes templates, resources and a glossary of export terms. 193 pages.

Sample export plans:

West Pacific Marketing Consultants
http://www.bplans.com/global_marketing_business_plan

Silvera & Sons
http://www.bplans.com/coffee_export_business_plan/

Grutzen Watches
http://www.bplans.com/export_watch_manufacturer_business_plan/

D.A.P. Exports [automobile parts]
http://www.bplans.com/export_automobile_parts_business_plan/

(Find other business plans at *http://www.bplans.com*)

2b. Exporting to Europe

Exporting to the EU – A Guide for Canadian Business
http://tradecommissioner.gc.ca/european-union-europeenne/market-facts-faits-sur-le-marche/0000256.aspx

> Trade Commissioner Service. Contents include customs, EU sanitary and phytosanitary requirements, product safety, packaging and labelling, EU consumer rights, intellectual property, government (public) procurement and business travel. 56 pages.

Canada-European Union Comprehensive Economic & Trade Agreement
http://www.international.gc.ca/gac-amc/campaign-campagne/ceta-aecg/index.aspx

> Government of Canada. Main page promotes the benefits of the Canada-EU CETA. Includes an overview of the benefits to 12 key industry sectors in Canada and links to country information on the Trade Commissioner Service's website.

The Nitty-Gritty of EU Trade Barriers Before and After CETA
https://edc.trade/eu-trade-barriers

> Export Development Canada. Overview of tariff and non-tariff barriers, quotas, licensing, customs clearance, procurement, product classifications, and rules of origin. July 2017.

Understanding the Four Faces of Europe: Preparing for Freer Commerce
http://www.conferenceboard.ca/e-library/abstract.aspx?did=7370

> Conference Board of Canada. This briefing identifies four European country groupings, each presenting pros and cons for Canadian businesses. The groupings are based on economic and business criteria: integrated value chain grouping of Germany and its Eastern European neighbours; the global niche players of Northern Europe; the inward-looking large consumer markets such as France; and the UK's services-led model. 46 pages, 2015. (Registration required.)

Doing Business 2017 – European Union (EU)
http://www.doingbusiness.org/reports/~/media/WBG/DoingB
usiness/Documents/Profiles/Regional/DB2017/EU.pdf

> World Bank. Overall in the EU, Denmark ranks highest in ease of doing business and Malta lowest. Other indicators show that France has the highest tax rate (% of profit) and Luxembourg the lowest; indicators measuring the time and cost for documentary compliance and border compliance to export and import show that Ireland ranks lowest within the EU with respect to ease of trading across borders. 387 pages.

Trade Helpdesk
http://trade.ec.europa.eu/tradehelp

> European Commission. Written for developing countries. Sections include requirements & taxes, EU import requirements, VAT rules & excise duties, import tariffs, 10-digit HS codes, trade statistics, and business contacts, including customs & taxation organizations. Click on "Requirements" to retrieve product-specific requirements; click on "European Market" to find import requirements in the target European country.

Your Europe
http://europa.eu/youreurope/business

> European Commission. Subtitled "Practical guide to doing business in Europe," this portal gives access to many regulations of interest to companies targeting the European Union market, such as VAT rules, competition rules, product requirements and energy labels.

Country Commercial Guides
https://www.export.gov/ccg

US Dept. of Commerce. Written for US exporters. Provides European Union market overview, challenges, opportunities and market entry strategy. In particular, the middle chapter covers trade regulations, customs and standards. There is a single CCG for the European Union, and also separate CCGs for specific countries in Europe: Albania, Austria, Belgium, Bosnia Herzegovina, Bulgaria, Croatia, Cyprus, Czech Republic, Denmark, Estonia, Finland, France, Germany, Greece, Hungary, Iceland, Ireland, Italy, Latvia, Macedonia, Malta, Montenegro, Netherlands, Norway, Poland, Portugal, Romania, Serbia, Slovakia, Slovenia, Spain, Sweden, Turkey, Ukraine, and the UK.

Market Access Guides – Europe
https://www.enterprise-ireland.com/en/Publications/Market-Access-Guides

Enterprise Ireland. Guides to exporting to Benelux countries: France, Great Britain, Italy, the Nordic region, Poland, Spain, Switzerland and Turkey. Typical contents include critical success factors, starting in the market, routes to market, tax and legal issues, growth sectors, and selling to the government.

Exporting to Austria
http://www.advantageaustria.org/ca/zentral/business-guide-oesterreich/exportieren-nach-oesterreich.en.html

Advantage Austria. Topics include market and consumers, sales distribution channels and transport, foreign traders ("transit"), advertising & media, financing, import regulations, contracts, terms & conditions, and standards & commercial law.

Doing Business in Denmark
https://www.export.org.uk/page/Denmark_Guide

Institute of Export & International Trade. Written for UK exporters. Contents include information on sector-specific opportunities, how to prepare to export, details on business etiquette & culture, and material on trade shows. 104 pages, 2017 (advertiser supported).

ixPOS, Your Business in Germany
http://www.ixpos.de

Germany Trade & Invest. MarketPlace Germany describes the infrastructure, federal states, and business travel. Market Entry covers tax and duty, import regulations, standards and distribution channels. Business Sectors provides statistics, market access issues and distribution channels for nine industry sectors: automotive, chemicals, consumer goods, machinery and equipment, medical technology, metal and metal processing, renewable energy, and service industries.

Doing Business in Ireland
https://www.export.org.uk/page/Ireland_Guide

Institute of Export & International Trade. Written for UK exporters. Contents include information on sector-specific opportunities, how to prepare to export, details on business etiquette & culture, and material on trade shows. 100 pages, 2016 (advertiser supported).

Doing Business in Poland
https://www.export.org.uk/page/Poland_Guide

Institute of Export & International Trade. Written for UK exporters. Contents include information on sector-specific opportunities, how to prepare to export, details on business etiquette & culture, and material on trade shows. 112 pages, 2017 (advertiser supported).

Doing Business in Romania
https://www.export.org.uk/page/Romania_Guide

Institute of Export & International Trade. Written for UK exporters. Contents include information on sector-specific opportunities, how to prepare to export, details on business etiquette & culture, and material on trade shows. 112 pages, 2016 (advertiser supported).

Sweden Market Entry Guide
http://www.sacc-usa.org/export-guides/doing-business-in-sweden/sweden-market-entry-guide

Swedish-American Chambers of Commerce. Written for US exporters. Covers finding your micro market, competition, and customs tariffs & taxes.

3. Market research basics

You have probably done secondary research in the past on your domestic market, perhaps without even realizing it. The types of questions needing answers, and types of resources that you used, will not have been very different from those you'll use when researching your potential export market. But if you are new to the concept, or those earlier research efforts are a distant memory, subsection 3a includes some useful introductions and reminders.

Ready-made reports are available occasionally, from sources described in subsection 3b. These include brief market overviews provided by government agencies in their exporter support programs, and comprehensive commercial market surveys. Even if these ready-made reports are too broad for your current needs, or too expensive, they offer a useful guide to the type of questions you should be asking and possible sources for the answers.

In addition to providing some market overviews, the federal and provincial governments, and some non-profit agencies, have funding programs that include market research and marketing among the eligible activities. These are described in subsection 3c, along with directories of research services that you could engage to complement your own research. See also Section 6 for sector-specific funds and programs.

Use subsection 3d Countries – quick facts to start building your own overview of the target export market, or to update the data you found in a guide to exporting. Then use the resources in subsection 3e to supplement those figures with more current or specific economic and trade data, from the European Union (EU) statistics system and the statistical agencies of individual countries in Europe, both within and outside the EU.

National trade and investment agencies publish profiles of important industry sectors in their countries, as described in subsection 3f. For sectors which represent your customers or your competitors, the profiles will be useful for finding statistics about the industry, the location of regional clusters, and key government organizations in the sector.

3a. Getting started

Conducting Market Research
https://canadabusiness.ca/business-planning/market-research-and-statistics/conducting-market-research

> Canada Business Network. A useful overview of the market research process, though not specific to international trade. Includes guide to market research and analysis, designing a questionnaire, types of survey questions, market research methods, and international market research.

Principles of Marketing Tutorials
https://www.knowthis.com/principles-of-marketing-tutorials

> KnowThis LLC. Tutorials on market research cover planning and primary and secondary research. Under "Manage and Plan", see also tutorials on preparing a market study, and writing a marketing plan.

SBA Export Business Planner
Chapter 4: Creating an export business plan
https://www.sba.gov/sites/default/files/SBA%20Export%20Bu siness%20Planner.pdf

US Small Business Administration. Written for US small businesses. Includes these worksheets: market expansion – benefits/trade-offs; business analysis; industry analysis; products with export potential; matching products to global trends/needs; most penetrable markets; markets to pursue; and short- and long-term goals.

SBA Export Business Planner
Chapter 5: Developing your marketing plan
https://www.sba.gov/sites/default/files/SBA%20Export%20Bu siness%20Planner.pdf

US Small Business Administration. Written for US small businesses. Includes these worksheets: market factor assessment; your industry in target global markets; building a distributor or agent relationship; marketing your product/service; marketing your product – identifying practical needs; defining your marketing strategy; and identifying customers within your chosen markets.

Interactive Marketing Plan
https://www.desjardins-business-tools.com/interactive-marketing-plan

Desjardins. This planning tool provides a methodology to help you build your market research, target your audience, analyze your competitors, determine the strengths and weaknesses of your business and predict the opportunities and threats it may face.

3b. Ready-made reports

Market Reports
http://www.tradecommissioner.gc.ca (under Export, click on Market Reports)

Trade Commissioner Service. Brief overviews of specific market sectors, for example Bioenergy Sector Profile – Sweden. Additional information on business conditions, for example Customs & Customs Formalities – France. Browse by country or industry sector. (Registration required.)

Top Markets Series
http://trade.gov/topmarkets

US International Trade Administration. Written for US exporters, the reports rank future export opportunities within 27 industries: agricultural equipment, aircraft parts, automotive parts, building products and sustainable construction, civil nuclear, cloud computing, cold supply chain, construction equipment, defense products, education, environmental technologies, financial technology, franchising, health IT, industrial automation, manufacturing technology, media and entertainment, medical devices, oil and gas, pharmaceuticals, recreational transportation, renewable energy, renewable fuels, semiconductors and related equipment, smart grid, technical textiles, and travel and tourism. Each industry report provides a market assessment of the competitiveness, opportunities and challenges within a sector, and case studies.

Euromonitor Reports
http://www.euromonitor.com/store

Euromonitor. Global market research database of statistics and research reports, providing insight on industries, economies and consumers worldwide. Free examples of reports and data sets, free table of contents and executive summary of specific report; purchase complete report. ($)

MarketResearch.com
http://www.marketresearch.com

A collection of market intelligence reports from over 720 publishers. Browse by category or search by specific product. Free abstract and table of contents, and search inside the report; purchase complete report. ($)

Research and Markets
https://www.researchandmarkets.com

Research "store", offering commercial reports from 1700 publishers – market reports, company reports, etc. Table of contents free, purchase complete report. ($)

3c. Support for market research

CanExport
http://international.gc.ca/canexport

Global Affairs Canada. The program supports Canadian SMEs that are seeking new export opportunities, particularly in high-growth markets, reimbursing up to 50% of eligible expenses for initiatives to develop new markets, including activities such as doing market research or participating in trade fairs. Non-repayable contributions from the program will be $10,000-$99,999 per project.

Export Market Access
http://exportaccess.ca/en/home

Ontario Chamber of Commerce. Grants available include conducting market research for more precise international market targeting, direct contacts at international trade shows and trade missions, and foreign bidding projects.

Aboriginal Business and Entrepreneurship Development Program
http://www.aadnc-aandc.gc.ca/eng/1375201178602/1375202816581

Indigenous and Northern Affairs Canada. The program is delivered through aboriginal financial institutions; it covers local, domestic, or export oriented marketing initiatives.

Adam Chowaniec Memorial Fund for Global Entrepreneurship
http://www.startupcan.ca/adam-chowaniec-memorial-fund-for-global-entrepreneurship

Startup Canada, on behalf of Export Development Canada. Grants to individuals, groups and organizations to build up the export and international capability of Canadian entrepreneurs. Project examples may include trade missions, global ecosystem tours, soft landings programs, export training bootcamps and global partnership facilitation.

BDC Xpansion Loan
https://www.bdc.ca/en/financing/business-loans/pages/expansion-loan.aspx

Business Development Bank of Canada. For projects such as expanding your market, launching a new marketing campaign, applications to protect your intellectual property, or obtaining a certification. BDC also offers an international business development consulting service.

FedNor – Innovation Fund
http://fednor.gc.ca/eic/site/fednor-fednor.nsf/eng/fn03444.html

FedNor. Support for a) R&D with commercial market potential (for example, early stage marketing, product certifications, and market research to direct future R&D) and b) activities to increase the level of competitiveness in key sectors, such as biotechnology, mining, forest industries, agri-food, ICT, renewable energy and manufacturing.

Global Opportunities for Associations
http://tradecommissioner.gc.ca/funding-financement/goa-oma

Trade Commissioner Service. Support for national associations undertaking international business development activities, in strategic markets and sectors, for the benefit of an entire industry.

Investing in Business Growth and Productivity
http://www.feddevontario.gc.ca/eic/site/723.nsf/eng/h_0186 7.html

FedDev Ontario. Funding for businesses to grow through market diversification and expanding facilities, or increase business capacity to participate in global markets through integration in global value chains. For SMEs, not-for-profit industry associations and regional economic development organizations.

Northern Ontario Productivity Assessments – SMART North
http://www.cme-smart.ca/fednor-en

Canadian Manufacturers & Exporters, for FedNor. CME's SMART program can contribute 50% of the eligible costs to a maximum of $15,000 to help Northern Ontario companies identify opportunities in product and process improvements, including market analysis.

Southern Ontario Fund for Investment & Innovation
http://www.sofii.ca

Community Futures Ontario. A loan fund for businesses in Southern Ontario addresses growth challenges including expansion into new markets.

Southwestern Ontario Development Fund
http://www.ontario.ca/southwesternfund

Ontario Government. The fund is for existing businesses and economic developers in southwestern Ontario. Eligible projects would enhance productivity and competitiveness; create high-value, sustainable jobs; increase exports; and promote a culture of innovation. Businesses apply under the "Business Stream".

Grants and Financing
http://canadabusiness

Canada Business Network. Links to government grants and financing, private sector financing, and accessing equity financing. Not specific to international trade, but a useful overview of general sources of business financing.

Find Funding
https://concierge.innovation.gc.ca/en/find-funding

National Research Council of Canada, Concierge Service. Click on "Market development: domestic and international" to identify export-related funding programs.

Canadian Small Business Funding Guide
https://web.mentorworks.ca/funding-guide

Mentor Works. Contents include sources of Canadian government funding, how to qualify for funding programs, how recipients obtain funds, document preparation tips, how to receive maximum value grants and loans, and how to get started with government funding applications. (Registration required.)

ESOMAR Directory of Research
https://directory.esomar.org

> ESOMAR. ESOMAR is an international market research association with 5000 individual members in 130 countries, particularly in Europe; the Directory of Research includes a directory of research companies.

3d. Countries – quick facts

Country Information
http://www.edc.ca (click on Country Info)

> Export Development Canada. Search by country to find overviews covering economic and political issues.

Global Export Forecast
http://www.edc.ca (from Knowledge Centre menu, click on Economic Analysis & Research)

> Export Development Canada. Which foreign markets will offer the best opportunities for Canadian exporters in the coming year; sales outlook by sector; major risks faced by exporters.

Country Risk Quarterly
http://www.edc.ca (from Knowledge Centre menu, click on Economic Analysis & Research)

> Export Development Canada. Risks and opportunities of doing business in over 100 countries, including Croatia, the Czech Republic, Estonia, France, Germany, Greece, Hungary, Italy, Lithuania, Poland, Portugal, Romania, Serbia, Spain, Turkey, Ukraine and the UK.

UNECE Countries in Figures
http://w3.unece.org/PXWeb/en/PDFCountryProfiles

UN Economic Commission for Europe. Latest demographic and economic data for 54 countries, mostly Europe but also Canada and the US. 2 pages for each country.

UNCTADstat Country Profiles
http://unctadstat.unctad.org/CountryProfile/GeneralProfile/e n-GB/004/index.html

UN Conference on Trade & Development. Statistical summaries of merchandise trade, trade in services, and economic trends. Browse by country. Click on Data Center for more detailed statistical reports, such as currency exchange rates or inflation rates.

BBC Country Profiles
http://news.bbc.co.uk/2/hi/country_profiles/default.stm

BBC. History, politics and economic background of countries and territories and background on key institutions, plus audio and video clips from BBC archives. Search by country or territory.

CIA World Factbook
https://www.cia.gov/library/publications/the-world-factbook

US Central Intelligence Agency. Brief information on history, people, government, economy, energy, geography, communications, and transportation for 267 countries. Also provides maps and country comparisons.

Country Insights
http://www.international.gc.ca/cil-cai/country_insights-apercus_pays/countryinsights-apercuspays.aspx

Global Affairs Canada, Centre for Intercultural Learning. Links to country-specific topics, including the economy and media and cultural topics: from conversations and communication styles to relationship building and stereotypes.

FITA Country Profiles and Resources
http://fita.org/countries/eur.html

Federation of International Trade Associations. Links to resources for 43 European countries. Brief introductory information and separate sections on business environment, economic/political overview, selling and buying, operating a business, investing, and travelling.

ESO European Sources Online
http://www.europeansources.info/search.jsp (under Information Guides, click on European Countries and Regions)

European Documentation Centre, Cardiff University. For each country, a one-page summary provides content and updating record. Click on "Source URL" to reach the guide, which contains frequently-checked links to a wide range of sources.

GlobalEdge Insights by Country
https://globaledge.msu.edu/global-insights (select a country)

Michigan State University. Links to sources of information by country. Also includes statistics, economy, history, government, culture, risk, corporations, trade statistics, indices, and other resources.

Export Business Map
https://customers.withgoogle.com/canada

Google. Summaries of data from the top ten export countries, including seasonality calendars showing important holidays, and facts about web and mobile usage. The Canada version includes Belgium, Italy, Netherlands and the UK; the Belgium version also includes France, Germany, Poland, Spain and Switzerland; the British version also includes Austria and Sweden.

3e. Statistics sources

Eurostat
http://ec.europa.eu/eurostat

EC Statistical Office of the European Commission. Under "General and regional statistics", click on "Regions" to find statistics for countries and smaller regions (counties, länder, etc.). Other sections include Industry and International trade, among others.

Statistics Explained – Your guide to European statistics
http://ec.europa.eu/eurostat/statistics-explained/index.php/Main_Page

Eurostat. This official Eurostat website presents statistical topics in an easily understandable way. Together, the articles make up an encyclopedia of European Union statistics, with numerous links to further information and the latest data and metadata, as a portal for occasional users. Browse articles by theme, such as economy & finance, industry & services, etc.

National Statistical Offices Websites
https://unstats.un.org/home/nso_sites

United Nations. Links to all national statistical offices, such as Instituto Nacional de Estadística of Spain.

International Statistical Agencies
https://www.census.gov/population/international/links/stat_i nt.html

US Census Bureau. Links to statistical agencies worldwide including European countries, from Albania Institute of Statistics to UK Statistics Authority and the General Register Office for Scotland.

Trade Data Online
http://www.ic.gc.ca/tdo

Innovation, Science & Economic Development Canada. Trade data from Statistics Canada and US Census Bureau. Search for exports or imports by industry (NAICS codes) or by product (HS codes). Choose national or provincial detail and country of origin or destination. Has a useful search tool for finding HS or NAICS codes.

Trade Map Canada
http://www.trademap.org/canada

UN/WTO International Trade Centre. Indicators on export performance, international demand, alternative markets and competitive markets, in the form of tables, graphs and maps, and a directory of trading companies. Covers 220 countries and 5300 products of the Harmonized System (HS). Monthly, quarterly and yearly trade flows are available down to the tariff line level (8 digits).

OECD.Stat
http://stats.oecd.org

OECD. A wide range of statistics allowing comparison between Canada and 26 European countries. Series include consumer and producer price indices, business statistics by industry classification, urban economic statistics, and ICT use by businesses.

UNdata
http://data.un.org

United Nations. 34 databases covering economic and socio-demographic topics, from crime and education to tourism and trade, for countries around the world. Descriptions of the international sources and definitions used in compiling the data are included. Sources include UN, FAO, IMF, OECD, UNESCO, WTO, WHO, and other international agencies.

World DataBank
http://databank.worldbank.org

World Bank. Development data covering 1157 indicators, 249 countries, and 18 regional and income groups, such as population, income, social, economic, financial, natural resources, and the environment. Country Group search available for Western Europe and European Union. Left panel provides search options; right panel displays preview of data.

International Data Base
https://www.census.gov/population/international/data/idb/info
rmationGateway.php

> US Census Bureau. Provides demographic indicators and population growth estimates for countries, pre-determined regions such as least developed countries, and custom groupings.

Trade & Tariff Data
https://www.wto.org/english/res_e/statis_e/statis_e.htm

> World Trade Organization. Home page for statistical series from WTO: merchandise trade, tariff databases, and environmental policy database.

Trade Profiles 2016
https://www.wto.org/english/res_e/publications_e/trade_profiles16_e.htm

> World Trade Organization. Major exports and imports are listed for agricultural and non-agricultural products, and also for major origins and destinations (with EU28 counted as a single trading destination). Trade in services provides a detailed breakdown for transport, travel and other commercial services. Also covers foreign affiliate statistics and intellectual property statistics. 400 pages, 2016.

I-TIP Goods
http://i-tip.wto.org/goods

> WTO Integrated Trade Intelligence Portal. Comprehensive information on non-tariff measures applied by WTO members in merchandise trade. It includes technical barriers to trade, sanitary and phytosanitary measures, and anti-dumping and countervailing measures. Customs valuation, rules of origin and import licences to be added in 2017.

I-TIP Services
http://i-tip.wto.org/services

WTO Integrated Trade Intelligence Portal. Search Statistics to find trade in US$ millions, by individual countries or "all members" (displays country by country), and for sectors and subsectors, such as R&D services and news agency services. Find sector-specific indicators available, such as hospital beds and mobile cellular telephone subscriptions.

Services Trade for Principal Partners
http://www.international.gc.ca/economist-economiste/statistics-statistiques/principal_partners-principaux_partenaires.aspx

Global Affairs Canada. Annual data on service exports and imports between Canada and its principal partners. Published in July.

Legatum Prosperity Index
http://www.prosperity.com

Legatum Institute. Index of countries based on business environment, economic quality, education, governance, health, natural environment, personal freedom, safety & security, and social capital. Browse by rankings, use the interactive data tool, or download 4- to 5-page country reports.

3f. Sector summaries

Emerging Europe – Key Sector Opportunities
http://emerging-europe.com/key-sector-opportunities

Emerging Europe. EM is an online magazine focused on Central & Eastern Europe. From this page, link to sector summaries and articles on aerospace, automotive, chemical, construction, creative, defence, financial services, food, furniture, gas & petroleum, health, ICT, engineering, media, mining, energy, retail, infrastructure, textiles tourism and logistics industries.

Austria – Fresh View
http://www.advantageaustria.org/international/zentral/fresh-view.en.html

Advantage Austria. Substantial material on Austrian exporting sectors: renewable energy, aviation technologies, traffic infrastructure, organic food, smart cities, environmental technology, life sciences & medical technology, machinery & plant construction, sustainable building, plastics, tourism infrastructure, education, and design.

Belgium – Sectoral Publications
http://abh-ace.be/en/importers/sectoral_publications

Belgian Foreign Trade Agency. Substantial publications on biotechnology, software, advanced materials, sustainable energy solutions, waste & recycling solutions, innovative food solutions, digital banking technologies, and cosmetics.

Croatian Industries
http://www.investincroatia.hr

Croatian Chamber of Economy. Brief brochures on food processing, ICT, manufacturing, metal processing, pharmaceutical, textile, wood processing & furniture manufacturing, and tourism industries.

Czech Republic – Target Sectors
http://www.czechinvest.org/en/target-sectors

CzechInvest. Brochures on nanotechnology & advanced materials, automotive industry, aerospace, energy & environment, life sciences, high-tech mechanical engineering, ICT, business support services, electronics & electrical engineering, and data centres.

Danish Key Industries
http://www.investindk.com/Clusters

Invest in Denmark. Industry profiles of cleantech, ICT, life sciences, maritime, design and food sectors.

Finland – Business Opportunities
http://www.investinfinland.fi/business-opportunities

FinPro. Brief overviews for ICT & digitalization, health & well-being, cleantech, and bioeconomy, and 2-page brochures for subsectors, e.g. gaming, wearables, digital health technologies, smart grid and wood construction.

Les Pôles de Compétitivité [France]
http://competitivite.gouv.fr/home-903.html

Direction Générale des Entreprises. Profiles of more than 70 competitiveness clusters in France. Identify industry clusters from a map, or filter by region or industry sector.

Industries in Germany
https://www.gtai.de/GTAI/Navigation/EN/Invest/industries.html

Germany Trade & Invest. From this home page, find industry and market numbers, and link to the latest publications, for 15 sectors, from automotive & aviation to materials processing & technologies.

Latvia – Sectors and Industries
http://www.liaa.gov.lv/en/invest-latvia/sectors-and-industries

LIAA Investment & Development Agency of Latvia. Brief overviews with links to publications and agencies, for woodworking, metalworking & mechanical engineering, transport & storage, IT & business services, environmental technology, healthcare, life sciences and food processing.

Netherlands – Key Sectors
https://www.hollandtradeandinvest.com/key-sectors

Holland Trade and Invest. Detailed overviews of industries and clusters in agriculture & food, creative industries, chemical industry, energy, high tech, horticulture, life science & health, logistics and water.

Industries in Norway
http://www.innovasjonnorge.no/en/start-page/invest-in-norway/industries

> Innovation Norway. Brief overviews of industries with links to clusters, for bioeconomy, data centres, electric mobility, energy & cleantech, healthcare, manufacturing & process industries, maritime, oil & gas, and travel & tourism.

Poland – Sectors
http://www.paih.gov.pl/sectors

> Polish Investment & Trade Agency. Brief industry overview and links to clusters in aerospace, automotive, biotechnology, business support services, domestic appliances, electronics, food processing, IT, renewable energy and R&D.

Romania – Strategic Sectors
http://investromania.gov.ro/web/business-in-romania

> InvestRomania. Brief overviews and links to presentations on ICT, automotive, aerospace, agriculture, bio-industry and creative industry.

Slovenia – Industries
https://www.investslovenia.org/industries/

> Invest Slovenia. Brief overview and links to leading companies in automotive, chemicals & pharmaceuticals, ICT, logistics & distribution, machinery & metalworking, and wood processing.

Spain – Sectors
http://www.investinspain.org/invest/en/sectors/index.html

ICEX – Invest in Spain. Overview, business opportunities, documents and case studies for aerospace, automotive, life sciences, ICT and chemical sector.

Sweden – Sector Overviews
http://business-sweden.se/en/Invest/Inspiration/publications

Business Sweden. Brochures on sectors: bioeconomy, cleantech, contact centres, life sciences, etc.

Switzerland – Sectors
http://s-ge.com/en/sectors

Switzerland Global Enterprise. Fact sheets on key sectors: food, ICT, life sciences, MEM (mechanical, electrical & metal), biotech, medtech, chemical & pharmaceutical, cleantech, and links to other sectors such as banking and design.

Turkey – Sectors
http://www.invest.gov.tr/en-US/sectors/Pages/Sectors.aspx

Invest in Turkey. Overviews leading to substantive reports on major sectors: agriculture & food, automotive, business services, chemicals, energy & renewables (incl. environmental technologies), financial services, ICT & electronics, life sciences, machinery & manufacturing, mining & metals, real estate and transport & logistics (incl. infrastructure).

London's Economic Plan
http://www.uncsbrp.org

The London Plan. This website provides a wealth of information on London's major industries including pharmaceutical and private healthcare; digital, media and technology industries; tourism, retail and fashion Industries; electronics, manufacturing and construction industries; and insurance, legal and financial industries.

Sector summaries are a quick way to get an overview of a customer group.

Looking at your own sector will provide ideas about in-market competitors and potential market entry partners. Find more sector-specific resources in **Section 6** of this toolbox.

4. Regulations and standards

4a. Export regulations & controls
4b. Intellectual property
4c. Standards, non-tariff trade barriers
4d. Taxes
4e. Doing Business In...

Canadian regulations require that exports be reported to the government. Certain products require Canadian certification, inspection or export permits (for example, food products require certification). Export controls cover military products, US technology, and dual-use items (goods and technology originally designed for civilian purposes, but that could have a military use). Some countries and foreign organizations are subject to Canadian sanctions. Resources describing these regulations are covered in subsection 4a.

Intellectual property rights are national in scope. Subsection 4b describes guides to intellectual property (IP), such as trademarks and designs, and resources for registering IP in target countries. Check also trademark databases to ensure that your proposed brand is not already registered to a competitor in that country – you may incur the expense of rebranding, but will avoid costly lawsuits.

Your product or service must meet standards requirements in the target market. Subsection 4c describes guides to national standards systems, non-tariff barriers to goods and services, and directories of standards organizations. See also Section 6 for regulations and guides that are sector-specific.

Local sales taxes added to your product or service will impact the cost to the final consumer. Income tax obligations such as withholding tax, business registration taxes and other taxes impact the cost of exporting. Subsection 4d includes guides to foreign income and sales taxes, for both countries within the EC Taxation and Customs Union, and other countries in Europe. See also subsection 8a, which includes guides to customs duties.

Finally, subsection 4e in this regulatory section describes general guides covering the legal, tax and other issues associated with doing business in European countries, including investments such as establishing branch offices, etc. Some guides may include summaries of import/export regulations. There are many other such guides – this selection includes the most recent and comprehensive.

4a. Export regulations & controls

Exporting Regulations
https://canadabusiness.ca/government/regulations/regulated -business-activities/exporting-regulations

> Canada Business Network. Summarizes export regulations, such as having a Business Number with an import-export account, and gives examples of what is needed to comply with import regulations of the target country.

A Step-by-Step Guide to Exporting Commercial Goods from Canada
http://www.cbsa-asfc.gc.ca/export/guide-eng.html

> Canada Border Services Agency. An overview of the exporting process, explaining the Canadian customs regulations and programs covered by CBSA's Memoranda Series D1 to D22.

Checklist for Exporting Commercial Goods from Canada
http://www.cbsa.gc.ca/export/checklist-controle-eng.html

Canada Border Services Agency. Steps to be compliant with CBSA regulations on exports, from obtaining an import/export business number to completing and submitting the export declaration electronically.

Export and Import Controls
http://www.international.gc.ca/controls-controles/index.aspx

Global Affairs Canada. Export control information for softwood lumber, agri-food products, textiles and clothing, steel, military & strategic technology, goods and technology of US origin, and miscellaneous goods (includes dual-use goods).

Export Controls Handbook
http://www.international.gc.ca/controls-controles/military-militaires/handbook-manuel.aspx

Global Affairs Canada. The main reference tool on export controls. Sections include how to use the Export Control List, destination and origin considerations, the export permit application process, compliance with Export Controls, CBSA customs procedures, applications to export cryptographic items, and more.

Pocketbook on Canadian Export Controls
http://blg.com/en/NewsAndPublications/Documents/publication_2093.pdf

Borden Ladner Gervais LLP. Written as frequently asked questions (FAQs), such as What is an export permit? Does it matter if my product incorporates goods or technology of US origin? How long does it take to obtain an export permit? 14 pages, 2014.

Food Exports
http://www.inspection.gc.ca (*under* Food tab, click Exports)

Canadian Food Inspection Agency. CFIA verifies that exported food products meet Canadian requirements where applicable, as well as those of the importing country. This page provides information on exporting dairy products, eggs and egg products, fish and seafood, foods regulated under the Food and Drugs Act and Regulations, fresh fruits and vegetables, honey, meat and poultry products, and processed products (fruits, vegetables and maple products), as well as other foods manufactured in Canada.

Export Permits for Cryptographic Items
http://www.international.gc.ca/controls-controles/export-exportation/crypto/Crypto_Intro.aspx

Global Affairs Canada. Explains export permit applications for information security goods and technology, and for goods and technology employing cryptography. Cryptography controls are outlined in Group 1 (the Dual-Use List) of the Guide to Canada's Export Controls.

Other Government Departments and Agencies: Reference List for Exporters
http://www.cbsa-asfc.gc.ca/export/reflist-listeref-eng.html

Canada Border Services Agency. CBSA enforces export regulations on behalf of other federal government departments and agencies. This page lists some of the most commonly exported commodities that may require permits and/or certificates from other federal agencies. 2 pages.

CITES: Convention on International Trade in Endangered Species of Wild Flora and Fauna
http://www.ec.gc.ca/cites

Environment & Climate Change Canada. CITES protects endangered species worldwide. Any import, export or re-export of CITES-listed species must be authorized. For example, the export of wild American ginseng is prohibited in Canada – only cultivated American ginseng can be legally traded in Canada, and its export from Canada requires a Canadian CITES export permit.

Export and Import of Hazardous Waste and Hazardous Recyclable Material Regulations
http://www.ec.gc.ca/gdd-mw/default.asp?lang=En&n=39D0D04A-1 (under Guides)

Environment & Climate Change Canada. A Guide to Classification and a User Guide explain various aspects of the regulations.

Canadian Economic Sanctions
http://www.international.gc.ca/sanctions/index.aspx

Global Affairs Canada. Sanctions can impact your business by prohibiting trade and other economic activity with a foreign market. The sanctions imposed on specific countries, organizations or individuals vary, and may include export restrictions, technical assistance prohibition, etc.

4b. Intellectual property

Intellectual Property for Exporting Businesses
http://www.ic.gc.ca/eic/site/cipointernet-internetopic.nsf/eng/wr03073.html

> Canadian Intellectual Property Office. A guide to protecting your intellectual property, including trademarks. Provides links to resources under each step, including developing an IP strategy, searching IP databases in other countries, and protecting your rights.

SME Guides and Manuals
http://www.wipo.int/sme/en/documents/guides

> World Intellectual Property Organization. A series of guides for small business, for example "Exchanging value: Negotiating technology licensing agreements" and "In good company: Managing intellectual property issues in franchising".

Guide to Going Global: Intellectual Property and Technology
https://www.dlapiperintelligence.com/goingglobal/intellectual-property/

> DLA Piper. This guide outlines aspects of IPT laws relevant to businesses expanding globally. Covers 34 jurisdictions including Austria, Belgium, Czech Republic, Denmark, Finland, France, Germany, Hungary, Ireland, Italy, Luxembourg, Netherlands, Portugal, Spain, Sweden, Switzerland, Turkey and the UK. For each there is a summary of intellectual property rights, rights specific to patents, trademarks, copyrights, circuit layouts, and trade secrets, and key commercial contract considerations and contract terms. 292 pages, 2016.

IPR Charts and IP Guides
https://www.iprhelpdesk.eu/IP-Charts-IP-Guides

European IPR Helpdesk. Includes a short guide on EU trademark and a short guide on Community design.

Country IPR Toolkits
http://www.stopfakes.gov/business-tools/country-ipr-toolkits

US International Trade Administration. Detailed information on protecting and enforcing IPR in 20 countries including Croatia, the European Union, and Italy. Links to information provided by US embassies.

Turkey IP Country Factsheet
https://euipo.europa.eu/ohimportal/en/web/observatory/support-for-small-businesses

European Intellectual Property Office. Guide to protecting intellectual property in Turkey. Links to relevant laws and IP registration sites. 12 pages, 2014.

Ukraine IP Country Factsheet
https://euipo.europa.eu/ohimportal/en/web/observatory/support-for-small-businesses

European Intellectual Property Office. Covers trademarks, geographical indications, copyright, patents & designs, plant varieties and trade secrets. 30 pages, 2015.

How to Apply for a European Patent
https://www.epo.org/applying/basics.html

European Patent Office. Basic information about the steps involved in the European patent granting procedure, including application, filing & fees, search and fees, examination & fees, publication, granting, and validation.

European Patent Register
http://www.epo.org

European Patent Office. Contains all the publicly available procedural information on European patent applications as they pass through each stage of the granting process. It includes links to the patent registers of many of the EPO member states, showing the status of European patents after grant, when the national patent offices take over responsibility.

European TMDN databases [trademarks and designs]
https://euipo.europa.eu/ohimportal/en/databases

European Intellectual Property Office. In Europe, trademark protection can be granted through official trademark offices at national, international or European Community level, all of which can be searched in **TMView** database. Includes data from all EU Member States and the information available from WIPO. Check **Designview** for industrial designs.

Global Brand Database
http://www.wipo.int/branddb/en

World Intellectual Property Organization. Perform a trademark search by text or image in brand data, including trademarks, appellations of origin and official emblems. Data comes from multiple national and international sources.

UK Intellectual Property Office
https://www.gov.uk/government/organisations/intellectual-property-office

UK Intellectual Property Office. From this home page, link to separate sections on trademarks, patent, copyrights and designs. Click on "IP for Business" for a collection of guidance documents such as licensing intellectual property.

Directory of Intellectual Property Offices
http://www.wipo.int/directory/en/urls.jsp

World Intellectual Property Organization. Contact details of national copyright and industrial property offices worldwide.

Anti-Counterfeiting – A Global Guide 2017
http://www.worldtrademarkreview.com/Intelligence/Anti-counterfeiting/2017

World Trademark Review, A practical, country-by-country analysis of anti-counterfeiting procedure. Contents include industry insight, regional focus, and country chapters. Contains 3-page summaries of trademark law in 50 jurisdictions including Austria, Belgium, Germany, Greece, Italy, Romania, Turkey, Ukraine, and the UK.

Cross-Border Copyright Guide 2017
http://www.terralex.org/publication/f921a1f1e3/download?file id=3a71a22d86

TerraLex. Legislation and regulation, subsistence of copyright, ownership, infringement, remedies, enforcement and copyright reform. Countries covered include Denmark, France, Germany, Ireland, Italy, Lithuania, Netherlands, Norway, Spain, Sweden and the UK. 204 pages, Oct. 2016.

4c. Standards, non-tariff trade barriers

Standards Benefits for Industry
http://www.scc.ca/en/stakeholder-participation/orientation-modules/standards-benefits-for-industry

>Standards Council of Canada. Outlines how standards can help your business reach its global potential. Sections include preparing your business for export markets, understanding the impact of standards on your business, accessing the standards you need, verifying compliance or conformity to standards; and taking action.

Preparing Your Product for Export
https://www.export.gov/export-education

>US Trade Information Center. A chapter in "A Basic Guide to Exporting" covers branding/labelling & packaging, engineering & redesign, installation, product adaption, and warranties.

Export Quality Management: A Guide for Small and Medium-Sized Exporters
http://www.intracen.org/export-quality-management-a-guide-for-small-and-medium-sized-exporters-second-ed

>UN/WTO International Trade Centre. Written for exporters in developing countries. Covers quality control; technical requirements including standards, technical regulations, sanitary and phytosanitary measures; management systems; conformity assessment including testing, inspection and certification. 286 pages, 2011.

CE Marking
https://ec.europa.eu/growth/single-market/ce-marking/manufacturers_en

European Commission. By affixing the CE marking to a product, a manufacturer declares that the product meets all the legal requirements for CE marking and can be sold throughout the European Economic Area. Links from here to Directives for all product groups that require CE marking.

Six Steps to CE Marking
http://tradecommissioner.gc.ca/world-monde/133383.aspx

Trade Commissioner Service. The CE mark indicates that products meet all applicable European health, safety, performance and environmental requirements. The steps relate to finding the applicable CE Directive(s) and essential requirements, certification, documentation, and Declaration of conformity. (Registration required.)

GHS Implementation [chemicals]
https://www.unece.org/trans/danger/publi/ghs/implementation_e.html

UN Economic Commission for Europe. Country by country summary of implementation of Globally Harmonized System of Classification and Labelling of Chemicals (GHS) in areas such as transport, environment, occupational health and safety, and pesticides.

Guidance on Requirements for Substances in Articles
https://echa.europa.eu/guidance-documents/guidance-on-reach

European Chemicals Agency. REACH guidance for companies that import goods containing hazardous substances above 0.1% by weight. The guidance includes a summary of the regulatory obligations applicable to producers, importers and suppliers, and possible exemptions that may apply; a flowchart of the process shows whether and how substances in articles may be regulated. 109 pages, June 2017.

Database: European Customs Inventory of Chemical Substances
http://ec.europa.eu/taxation_customs/dds2/ecics/chemical substance_consultation.jsp

EC Taxation & Customs Union. Search the database to identify chemicals, classify them correctly in the combined nomenclature and name them in any EU language. The database covers pesticides listed by ISO, the International Nonproprietary Names assigned to pharmaceuticals by WHO, pharmaceuticals intermediates, narcotics and their precursors, ozone-depleting substances, toxic/dangerous chemicals controlled under the Chemical Weapons Convention, Colour Index dyes and pigments; and other commercially significant products.

Technical Barriers to Trade Database
http://ec.europa.eu/growth/tools-databases/tbt/en/search

European Commission. Technical barriers include mandatory product characteristics such as product size, weight, composition, packaging, and labelling; and conformity assessment procedures such as procedures for sampling, inspection, registration, or accreditation. Search this database by country, whether within or outside the EU, and by field of activity, such as healthcare or glass in building.

NTE Report on Foreign Trade Barriers
https://ustr.gov/sites/default/files/files/reports/2017/NTE/2017%20NTE.pdf

Office of the US Trade Representative. For each country except the US, describes trade barriers: import policies, sanitary and phytosanitary measures, government procurement, export subsidies, intellectual property, services barriers, investment barriers, anticompetitive activities, and e-commerce. 492 pages, annual.

Services Trade Restrictions Database
http://iresearch.worldbank.org/servicetrade/home.htm

World Bank. Comparable information on services trade policy measures for five sectors (telecommunications, finance, transportation, retail and professional services) and key modes of delivery. The data is presented in four ways: a single index of restrictiveness; a concise description of key restrictions; an annotated list of the important policy measures (restrictive or not); and a list of all policy measures for which data was collected. Country search options include EU-20, High income OECD, Europe and Central Asia, and some individual European countries.

Services Trade Restrictiveness Index
http://www.oecd.org/tad/services-trade/services-trade-restrictiveness-index.htm

> OECD. Country notes offer a 2-page analytical summary of services trade restrictiveness in each of 44 countries including Austria, Belgium, Czech Republic, Denmark, Estonia, Finland, France, Germany, Greece, Hungary, Iceland, Ireland, Italy, Latvia, Lithuania, Luxembourg, Netherlands, Norway, Poland, Portugal, Slovak Republic, Slovenia, Spain, Sweden, Switzerland, Turkey, and the UK. Sector Notes provide an analysis of the 18 different services sectors, from Accounting to Television and broadcasting. The Regulatory Database covers specific laws and regulations that contribute to services trade restrictiveness – filter by sector and country.

European Committee for Standardization – Search Standards
https://www.cen.eu/Pages/default.aspx

> Comité Européen de Normalisation. CEN is one of three European standardization organizations (together with CENELEC and ETSI) officially recognized by the EU and EFTA as being responsible for voluntary standards at European level. To search for standards by keyword or standards classification, click on the Search Standards tab.

Standards – National support & tools
https://www.cencenelec.eu/sme/NationalContacts/Pages/default.aspx

> CEN and CENELEC. SME Helpdesks are one-stop service points to introduce SMEs to the benefits of European Standards and to the business tools required to access the European Standardization System. This page provides contact information for national standards agencies in EU countries.

Technical Regulations Information System
http://ec.europa.eu/growth/tools-databases/tris/en

European Commission. Database or proposed national technical regulations. Member States must inform the Commission of any draft technical regulation prior to its adoption. From the date of notification of the draft, there is a three-month standstill period, during which the notifying Member State cannot adopt the technical regulation. Search by date, country, product category, or keyword.

Standards Alert!
https://www.scc.ca/en/standards/standards-alert

Standards Council of Canada. Subscribers receive e-mail updates about changes to the Canadian and international standards in a particular field of interest. Also allows users to track an individual standard.

Standards Store
https://www.standardsstore.ca

Standards Council of Canada. Provides a single point of entry to search and purchase standards and related publications from hundreds of standards developers around the world.

ISO Members
http://www.iso.org/iso/about/iso_members.htm

International Organization for Standardization. Profiles of national standards agencies, by country, with contact information and local websites.

4d. Taxes

Taxes in Europe
https://ec.europa.eu/taxation_customs/taxes-europe-database-tedb_en

> EC Taxation & Customs Union. The "Taxes in Europe" database (TEDB) covers the main taxes in force in the EU Member States, about 650 taxes. For each tax, the database describes its legal basis, assessment base, main exemptions, applicable rate(s), economic and statistical classification, and the revenue generated. Taxes include personal and corporate income taxes, value added taxes, EU harmonized excise duties, the main social security contributions, and other taxes yielding at least 0.1% of GDP, but not customs duties and tariffs.

National Tax Websites
https://ec.europa.eu/taxation_customs/national-tax-websites_en

> EC Taxation & Customs Union. Links to tax administration and ministry of finance in EU countries and candidate countries.

Worldwide Tax Guide 2017-18
http://www.pkf.com/publications/tax-guides/pkf-international-worldwide-tax-guide

> PKF International. Each country summary addresses the major taxes applicable to business; how taxable income is determined; the country's personal tax regime; and the Double Tax Treaty and Non-Treaty rates of tax withholding on royalties and other related payments. Countries include Austria, Belgium, Bulgaria, Cyprus, Czech Republic, Denmark, Estonia, Finland, France, Germany, Gibraltar, Greece, Guernsey, Hungary, Ireland, Isle of Man, Italy,

Jersey, Latvia, Luxembourg, Macedonia, Malta, Netherlands, Norway, Poland, Portugal, Romania, Serbia, Slovak Republic, Slovenia, Spain, Sweden, Switzerland, Turkey, Ukraine, and the UK. 942 pages, May 2017.

Tax Guides
https://dits.deloitte.com/#TaxGuides

Deloitte. Taxation and investment guides for Austria, Belgium, Cyprus, Denmark, Finland, France, Germany, Hungary, Ireland, Italy, Luxembourg, Netherlands, Norway, Poland, Spain, Sweden, Switzerland, Ukraine, and the UK. Sections include investment climate, setting up a business, business taxation, withholding taxes, indirect taxes, taxes on individuals, labor environment. 30-35 pages, 2015-2017.

Guide to Going Global: Tax
https://www.dlapiperintelligence.com/goingglobal/tax

DLA Piper. This guide covers 22 jurisdictions including: Austria, Finland, France, Germany, Ireland, Italy, Luxembourg, Netherlands, Norway, Portugal, Spain, Sweden, Switzerland and the UK. The guide addresses common tax questions, including taxation of resident and non-resident companies, withholding taxes and employment tax.

Indirect Tax Country Guides
http://www.bakertillyinternational.com/web/country-guides.aspx

Baker Tilly International. Short summaries of sales taxes, VAT taxes and compliance obligations such as filing deadlines. Countries include Austria, Belgium, Bulgaria, Croatia, Cyprus, Czech Republic, Denmark, Estonia, Finland, France, Germany, Greece, Hungary, Ireland, Italy, Latvia, Lithuania, Luxembourg, Malta, Netherlands, Norway, Poland, Portugal, Romania, Slovak Republic, Slovenia, Spain, Sweden, Switzerland and the UK.

Global VAT Guide – Cross-border supplies of intangible services, rights and digital content
https://www.dlapiper.com/~/media/Files/Insights/Publication s/2016/05/Global_VAT_Guide_2016.pdf

DLA Piper. OECD VAT guidelines, tips for minimizing VAT (GST) risks for cross-border supplies, and sections on Finland, France, Germany, Italy, Luxembourg, Netherlands, Norway, Poland, Russia, Spain, Sweden and the UK. 56 pages, May 2016.

European VAT Refund Guide 2017
https://www2.deloitte.com/global/en/pages/tax/articles/vat-refund-guide.html

Deloitte. Businesses operating in countries in which they are not VAT-registered can incur significant amounts of local VAT on expenses paid. The guide summarizes the rules and how to reclaim VAT in 31 countries. 326 pages, 2017.

4e. Doing Business In...

World Bank Doing Business Project – Law Library
http://www.doingbusiness.org/law-library

World Bank. The Doing Business Project ranks countries for ease of doing business, by measures such as the time and documentation required in setting up a business or paying taxes. The Law Library is a searchable database of the regulations in specific countries, such as the Customs Tariff.

AmCham Business Index 2016-2017 [Albania]
http://www.amcham.com.al/wp-content/uploads/ 2017/03/AmCham-Business-Index-2016-2017.pdf

American Chamber of Commerce in Albania & Konsort Ltd. Perceptions of AmCham members on the business climate in Albania: overall tax level, government bureaucracy, monopoly and unfair competition, finding local qualified staff, and the informal economy. 56 pages, 2016.

Doing Business in Andorra
http://www.bakertillyinternational.com/media/2906021/doing-business-in-andorra.pdf

Baker Tilly International. Sections cover business entities & accounting, finance & investment, employment regulations, and taxation. 19 pages, 2016.

Austria: Guide to Doing Business
http://www.lexmundi.com/Document.asp?DocID=8625

LexMundi – CHSH. Sections on immigration requirements, investment climate, business structures, establishing a business, intellectual property, labour & employment, import and export regulations, and tax. 47 pages, July 2016.

Doing Business in Belgium
http://www.bakertillyinternational.com/media/2632743/doing-business-in-belgium.pdf

Baker Tilly International. Sections cover business entities & accounting, finance & investment, employment regulations, and taxation. 23 pages, Nov. 2016.

Belgium: Guide to Doing Business
http://www.lexmundi.com/Document.asp?DocID=6573

LexMundi – Liederkerke. Topics covered include investment incentives, financial facilities, exchange controls, import/export regulations, structures for doing business, establishment of a business, operation of the business, labour legislation and supply, tax system, immigration requirements, and expatriate employees. 87 pages, 2014.

Doing Business in Bosnia and Herzegovina
http://www.bakertillyinternational.com/media/2906096/doin
g-business-in-bosnia-and-herzegovina.pdf

> Baker Tilly International. Sections cover business entities
> & accounting, finance & investment, employment
> regulations, and taxation. 18 pages, April 2017.

Bulgaria: Guide to Doing Business
http://www.lexmundi.com/Document.asp?DocID=9087

> LexMundi – Penkov-Markov. Sections include investment
> incentives, exchange controls, import/export regulations,
> structures for doing business, labour legislation, taxes, and
> expatriate employees. 132 pages, 2017.

Doing Business in Croatia
http://www.scott-
moncrieff.com/assets/publications/Doing_business_in_Croatia
_2016.pdf

> Moore Stephens Europe. Sections include Croatia at a
> glance, doing business, finance & investment, accounting
> & audit environment, taxes on business, personal
> taxation, other taxes, and social security contributions. 48
> pages, Sept. 2016

Doing Business in Cyprus
https://www.moorestephens.com/publications/guides/doing-
business-in-cyprus-2016

> Moore Stephens. Sections include Cyprus at a glance, doing
> business, finance & investment, accounting & audit
> environment, taxes on business, personal taxation, other
> taxes, and social security contributions. 44 pages, Sept. 2016.

Doing Business in the Czech Republic
*http://www.bakermckenzie.com/en/insight/publications/2017
/02/dbi-czech-republic*

> Baker McKenzie. Sections include corporate registration &
> compliance, taxation, employment issues, real estate,
> environmental protection, competition rules, and product
> safety & consumer protection. 64 pages, Feb. 2017.

Doing Business in Denmark
*http://www.uhy.com/wp-content/uploads/Doing-Business-in-
Denmark_2016-2.pdf*

> UHY. Sections cover business environment, foreign
> investment, setting up a business, labour, taxation, and
> accounting & reporting. 31 pages, 2016.

Estonia: Guide to Doing Business
http://www.lexmundi.com/Document.asp?DocID=8721

> LexMundi – COBALT. Sections on investment, taxes,
> exchange controls, establishing a business, reporting
> requirements, operation of the business, competition,
> intellectual property, employment, expatriate employees,
> real estate, and dispute resolution. 67 pages, Aug. 2016.

Estonia – Business & Economy
http://www.estonianexport.ee/business

> Estonia Chamber of Commerce & Industry. This section of
> the chamber's website covers the Estonian economy at a
> glance, business environment, location – transport and
> logistics, foreign trade – importing and exporting, tax
> system and administration, labour market, e-Estonia, and
> business practices and culture.

Doing Business in Finland
https://www.moorestephens.com/publications/guides/doing-business-in-finland

Moore Stephens Rewinet OY. Sections include Finland at a glance, doing business, finance & investment, accounting & audit environment, taxes on business, personal taxation, other taxes, and social security contributions. 50 pages, 2015.

Doing Business in Finland
http://www.hlbi.com (click on Publications)

HLB International. Sections include investor requirements, types of business organizations, contract law, accounting & auditing, taxation, and value-added tax. 24 pages, Oct. 2016.

Doing Business in France
http://www.uhy.com/wp-content/uploads/Doing-Business-in-France-1.pdf

UHY. Sections cover business environment, foreign investment, setting up a business, labour, taxation, and accounting & reporting. 42 pages, 2017.

Doing Business in France
https://www.moorestephens.com/publications/guides/doing-business-in-france-2016

Moore Stephens – COFFRA. Sections include doing business, finance & investment, accounting & audit environment, taxes on business, personal taxation, other taxes, and social security contributions. 60 pages, July 2016.

Doing Business in Germany
http://www.business.hsbc.uk/en-gb/countryguide/germany

HSBC, with Grant Thornton. Chapters include country profile, legal overview, conducting business in Germany, tax system, labour, audit, trade, finance, and infrastructure. 37 pages, 2016.

Germany: Guide to Doing Business
http://www.lexmundi.com/Document.asp?DocID=8437

LexMundi – Noerr LLP. Sections on foreign investment, business vehicles, employment, tax, competition, intellectual property, marketing agreements, e-commerce, advertising, data protection, and product liability. 84 pages, 2015.

Doing Business in Greece
https://www.moorestephens.com/publications/guides/doing-business-in-greece2016

Moore Stephens. Sections include Greece at a glance, doing business, finance & investment, accounting & audit environment, taxes on business, personal taxation, other taxes, and social security contributions. 52 pages, July 2016.

Doing Business in Hungary
https://www.moorestephens.com/publications/guides/doing-business-in-hungary-2016

Moore Stephens. Sections include Hungary at a glance, doing business, finance & investment, accounting & audit environment, taxes on business, personal taxation, other taxes, and social security contributions. 64 pages, Aug. 2016.

Doing Business in Iceland
http://www.invest.is/files/skjol/doingbusiness.pdf

> Promote Iceland. Sections cover business & economy, foreign investment, establishing a business, labour force & employee benefits, taxation, and financial reporting & auditing. 59 pages, March 2017.

Doing Business in Ireland
http://www.business.hsbc.uk/en-gb/countryguide/ireland

> HSBC, with Grant Thornton. Chapters include legal overview, conducting business, tax system, labour, audit, trade, finance, and infrastructure. 35 pages, 2016.

Ireland: Guide to Doing Business
http://www.lexmundi.com/Document.asp?DocID=8755

> LexMundi – Arthur Cox. Sections include investment incentives, import/export regulations, structures for doing business, establishing & operating a business, labour, tax, immigration, and expatriate employees. 104 pages, 2015.

Doing Business in Italy
https://www.moorestephens.com/publications/guides/doing-business-in-italy-2016

> Moore Stephens – Studio Palma Debernardi Borghi e Associati. Sections include doing business, finance & investment, accounting & audit environment, taxes on business, personal taxation, other taxes, and social security contributions. 54 pages, Sept. 2016.

Doing Business in Latvia
https://www.moorestephens.com/publications/guides/doing-business-in-latvia

Moore Stephens. Sections include Latvia at a glance, doing business, finance & investment, accounting & audit environment, taxes on business, personal taxation, other taxes, and social security contributions. 42 pages, May 2017.

Doing Business in Lithuania
https://www.moorestephens.com/publications/guides/doing-business-in-lithuania-2016

Moore Stephens. Sections include doing business, finance & investment, accounting & audit environment, taxes on business, personal taxation, other taxes, and social security contributions. 36 pages, Jan. 2016.

Doing Business in Luxembourg
https://www.moorestephens.com/publications/guides/doing-business-in-luxembourg-2016

Moore Stephens. Sections include Luxembourg at a glance, doing business, finance & investment, accounting & audit environment, taxes on business, personal taxation, other taxes, and social security contributions. 42 pages, July 2016.

Guide to Doing Business & Investing in Macedonia
https://www.pwc.com/mk/en/about-us/doing_business_guide.html

PwC. Topics include country statistical profile, business environment, foreign investment, importing & exporting, business entities including local representation, and taxation. 56 pages, 2016.

Doing Business Guide – Malta
https://www.morisonksi.com/resources/view/826

Morison KSi. Topics include business structures, labour & personnel, taxation, banking & finance, reporting requirements, and sector opportunities. 18 pages, May 2017.

Doing Business in Malta
http://www.uhy.com/wp-content/uploads/Doing-Business-in-Malta.pdf

UHY. Sections cover business environment, foreign investment, setting up a business, labour, taxation, and accounting & reporting. 46 pages, 2015.

Doing Business in the Netherlands
http://www.bakermckenzie.com/en/insight/publications/2016/07/doing-business-in-the-netherlands

Baker McKenzie. Guide to the Dutch legal and taxation system. Topics include the main aspects of establishing a profitable firm, real estate, employment law, tax law and many other legal issues and regulations. 360 pages, July 2016.

Doing Business in the Netherlands
http://www.uhy.com/wp-content/uploads/Doing-Business-in-Netherlands-2016.pdf

UHY. Sections cover business environment, setting up a business, finding a location, subsidies, taxation, personnel, and accounting & reporting. 60 pages, April 2016.

Doing Business in Norway

http://www.uhy.com/wp-content/uploads/Doing-Business-in-Norway.pdf

UHY. Sections cover business environment, foreign investment, setting up a business, labour, taxation, and accounting & reporting. 23 pages, April 2016.

Doing Business in Poland

http://www.hlbi.com (click on Publications)

HLB International. Sections include investment factors, entrepreneurial environment, investment incentives, doing business in Poland, employment, social security, important regulations, taxation, corporate income tax, international tax issues, and VAT. 78 pages, Jan. 2017.

Doing Business in Portugal

https://www.moorestephens.com/publications/guides/doing-business-in-portugal-2016

Moore Stephens. Sections include doing business, finance & investment, accounting & audit environment, taxes on business, personal taxation, other taxes, and social security contributions. 48 pages, July 2016.

Doing Business in Romania

https://www.moorestephens.com/publications/landing-page-content/latest-guides/doing-business-in-romania-2015

Moore Stephens – SC Audit One. Sections include doing business, finance & investment, accounting & audit environment, taxes on business, personal taxation, other taxes, and social security contributions. 44 pages, June 2015.

Serbia: Guide to Doing Business
http://www.lexmundi.com/Document.asp?DocID=9013

LexMundi – JPM. Sections include exchange controls, import/export regulations, structures for doing business, establishing & operating the business, labour/employment, tax on corporations, immigration, and expatriate employees. 91 pages, 2016.

Doing Business in the Slovak Republic
http://www.bakermckenzie.com/en/insight/publications/2017 /02/dbi-slovak-republic

Baker McKenzie. Topics cover investment incentives, business entities, income tax, customs duties, audits & accounting, labour issues, real estate, foreign exchange, competition rules, environmental protection, register of public sector partners, and e-mail. 62 pages, Feb. 2017.

Slovenia: Guide to Doing Business
http://www.lexmundi.com/Document.asp?DocID=9016

LexMundi – Selhi & Partnerji. Sections include investment incentives, exchange controls, import/export regulations, structures for doing business, establishing & operating a business, labour, taxation, immigration, and expatriate employees. 73 pages, 2016.

Doing Business in Spain 2017
http://horwathhtl.com/2017/07/05/business-spain-2017/

Crowe Horwath. Covers incorporation in Spain, tax information, employment and social security, human resources, and visas. 44 pages.

Spain: Guide to Doing Business
http://www.lexmundi.com/Document.asp?DocID=9271

LexMundi – Uría Menéndez. Sections include business entities, investment regulations, trade regulations, distribution agreements, intellectual property and data protection, labour, and tax. 177 pages, Feb. 2016.

Doing Business in Sweden
http://www.uhy.com/wp-content/uploads/Doing-Business-in-Sweden.pdf

UHY. Sections cover business environment, foreign investment, setting up a business, labour, taxation, and accounting & reporting. 24 pages, 2015.

Doing Business in Switzerland
https://www.moorestephens.com/publications/guides/doing-business-in-the-switzerland-2016

Moore Stephens. Sections include Switzerland at a glance, doing business, finance & investment, accounting & audit environment, taxes on business, personal taxation, other taxes, and social security contributions. 40 pages, May 2016.

Turkey: Guide to Doing Business
http://www.lexmundi.com/Document.asp?DocID=8972

LexMundi – Pekin & Pekin. Sections include investment background, intellectual property, exchange controls, business structures, establishing & operating a business, labour relations, and tax. 52 pages, 2016.

Conducting Business in Ukraine
*http://www.bakermckenzie.com/-
/media/files/insight/publications/2017/conducting-business-
in-ukraine/conducting-business-in-ukraine-2017.pdf*

Baker McKenzie. Topics covered include foreign
investment; establishing a presence; anti-corruption
legislation; taxation; currency regulations; customs
regulations; property rights; privatization, competition
law; dispute resolution; financial services; capital markets;
employment; intellectual property; bankruptcy; consumer
protection and product liability; industry regulation; and
international trade and commerce. 351 pages, 2017.

Establishment of a Business in the UK by a Foreign Corporation
*https://www.hoganlovells.com/en/publications/establishment
-of-a-business-in-the-uk-by-a-foreign-corporation*

Hogan Lovells. A guide to the laws and taxes which will
apply to a foreign corporation establishing a business
operation in the UK and administrative requirements. 60
pages, July 2017.

Doing Business in the UK
http://www.business.hsbc.uk/en-gb/countryguide/uk

HSBC, with Grant Thornton. Chapters include country
profile, legal overview, conducting business in the UK, tax
system, labour, audit, trade, finance, and infrastructure.
34 pages, 2016.

ILLUSTRATION: Marc and Hazel would like to expand to Europe their successful line of sunscreen products for children.

Step 1: From resources in **Section 3b** they quickly find current research on the sun care market in European countries available from Mintel for US$600 per country.

Europe is the world's largest market for cosmetics & personal care products. Moreover, for EU countries there is a single regulation, from ingredients to labelling, and a single place to register the product – the Cosmetic Products Notification Portal. However, Marc and Hazel's business experience in Canada and subsequent expansion into the US market have given them an appreciation of the value of hiring experts to help in many aspects of market entry. So their *market research objective* is to determine which experts they might need.

Step 2: They begin their list with a trademark lawyer and marketing consultant, as intellectual property databases in **Section 4** show that they need new branding, to avoid infringement. For regulations for labelling and standards for retail packaging, they add experts in those areas to the list. They will need tax advice on both business income tax and sales tax/VAT.

Help with developing a market entry strategy goes to the very top of their list when they learn from the Cosmetics Europe website, **Section 6**, that there are 20,000 wholesalers plus 100,000 possible retail outlets in the EU.

Next step: In **Section 3c**, Marc and Hazel find that BDC has both a loan program to help them pay for their market expansion, and a consulting service to help them develop a market entry strategy.

5. Finding companies and organizations

5a. Multi-country directories
5b. Country-specific directories

The company directories in this section include incorporation registers, exporter directories, company databases, and rankings. Cluster organizations, industry associations and chambers of commerce also often have member directories.

Use these directories to identify potential customers, distributors, and competitors. More detailed directories may also be useful for finding suppliers of the products, components or services that you may need to source locally. More specific directories are described in Section 6 Sectors.

5a. Multi-country directories

EU Business Registers
https://e-justice.europa.eu/content_business_registers-104-en.do

European Justice. Since June 2017, business registers in all EU countries are interconnected. Click on "business registers at European level" to search by company name; click on "national business registers" to search by country for any EU(28) country and for Iceland, Liechtenstein and Norway (under INT).

Europages
http://www.europages.co.uk

Europages. Lists 2.6 million European companies by industry sector, geographic region, size and activity. Browse by one of 26 categories, or use keyword search and then restrict by country, size and category.

Kompass Online
https://www.kompass.com

> Kompass International. Database of 12 million companies in 60 countries. In the search box type keywords from product headings or from the company name, then filter by country, company size or other variable. Under "activities", company information shows the products and services, and whether the company is a manufacturer, distributor or service provider. Detailed company information and company lists are downloadable for a fee.

Trade Services Directory
http://www.globaltrade.net/expert-service-provider.html

> GlobalTrade.net. Directory of trade service providers worldwide, including banks, language services, lawyers, taxes, trade compliance and customs, trading companies and agents. Search by service category, country or keyword.

FT1000: Europe's Fastest Growing Companies
https://ig.ft.com/ft-1000

> Financial Times. Lists the 1000 companies in Europe that have achieved the highest percentage growth in revenues between 2012 and 2015. Ranking shows revenues, revenues growth, and employees. 78 companies are based in London; Paris is second with 45 companies, followed by Milan with 34 and Berlin with 32.

1000 Companies to Inspire – Europe
http://www.lseg.com/resources/1000-companies-inspire

> London Stock Exchange Group. 1000 of the fastest growing SMEs across the 28 countries of the European Union. Company profiles grouped by broad category: technology, food & drink, manufacturing & engineering, consumer services, and professional services.

Inc. 5000 Europe
https://www.inc.com/inc5000eu/list/2017

Inc. List of the fastest-growing private companies, based on three-year revenue growth. Under Advanced Search, sort by industry or country.

Emerging Europe Business Directory
http://emerging-europe.com/directory

Business Emerging Europe. Directory of companies in Central & Eastern Europe; browse by industry sector and country.

Deloitte Central Europe Top 500
https://www2.deloitte.com/global/en/pages/about-deloitte/articles/central-europe-top500.html

Deloitte. Ranks the 500 largest companies from the 18 countries in Central Europe and Ukraine, showing revenues and net income. Includes sector summaries for banking, consumer goods, energy & resources, insurance, manufacturing, and real estate & construction. 88 pages, 2016.

Deloitte Technology Fast 50 Central Europe
https://www2.deloitte.com/cefast50

Deloitte. Brief profiles of fast-growing companies in IT & digital solutions, media & telecommunications, and clean tech & energy. Companies are headquartered in Bosnia & Herzegovina, Bulgaria, Croatia, Czech Republic, Hungary, Lithuania, Poland, Romania, Serbia, Slovakia and Slovenia. 68 pages, 2016.

Top 100 SEE – SouthEast Europe's Biggest Companies
http://top100.seenews.com/wp-content/uploads/2012/07/SEE_top_100_2016_1.pdf

SeeNews. Series of "top 100" rankings show revenues and profits: companies, banks, insurers, and companies listed on local stock exchanges; "top 50" rankings of companies per capita (i.e. the importance of individual companies in their local economies) and most dynamic (i.e. revenue growth); and rankings of industry sectors by revenue and profit. Landscape section is "top 10" company rankings for Albania, Bosnia and Herzegovina, Bulgaria, Croatia, Macedonia, Moldova, Montenegro, Romania, Serbia, and Slovenia. 68 pages, 2016.

Global Business Directory
http://www.belgiumyp.com/international-business-directories-map

Publisher provides company business directories for Albania, Croatia, Cyprus, Estonia, Finland, Ireland, Lithuania, Luxembourg, Ireland, Malta, Netherlands, Norway, Poland, Portugal, Romania, Slovakia, Slovenia, Sweden, Switzerland, Turkey & the UK. Search by keyword for company or business category, or by location.

International Yellow Pages
http://www.yellowpages.dk/p/international-yellowpages

Links to telephone directories in Andorra, Austria, Belgium Bosnia and Herzegovina, Bulgaria, Croatia, Czech Republic, Estonia, Finland, France, Germany, Gibraltar, Greece, Hungary, Netherlands, Iceland, Ireland, Italy, Latvia, Lithuania, Luxembourg, Malta, Norway, Poland, Portugal, Romania, Serbia, Slovakia, Slovenia, Spain, Sweden, Switzerland, Turkey, Ukraine, and the UK.

List of Cluster Organizations
https://www.clustercollaboration.eu/cluster-list

European Cluster Collaboration Platform. Provides name, link and sector(s) scope of industry clusters in European countries. Search by country, then by sectoral industries from aerospace to wood products, by emerging industries such as advanced packaging and medical devices, and by technology fields, such as bio-composites and visualization.

World Directory of Importers Associations
http://www.intracen.org/itc/trade-support/importers-associations

UN/WTO International Trade Centre. Directory of more than 400 associations whose members are importers or provide support services to importers. Browse by country.

Directory of Trade Promotion Organizations and Other Trade Support Institutions (TSI Directory)
http://www.intracen.org/itc/trade-support/tsi-directory

UN/WTO International Trade Centre. Profiles of trade support organizations. Default arrangement is by country.

WCN World Chambers Directory
http://chamberdirectory.worldchambers.com

International Chamber of Commerce. Database of 12,000 chambers of commerce worldwide, for example the Northern Ireland Chamber of Commerce and Industry in Belfast and the Chambre de Commerce France-Canada in Paris. Provides contact details and links to websites and to member directories where available.

Eurochambres – Members
http://www.eurochambres.eu (under About Us, click on Our Members)

> Association of European Chambers of Commerce and Industry. Click on a printable "contact list", or link to a specific member, such as the Federation of Belgian Chambers of Commerce. Many of these local networks have business directories and guides to import, etc.

5b. Country-specific directories

WKO Firmen A-Z [Austria]
https://firmen.wko.at/Web/SearchComplex.aspx

> Wirtschaftskammer Österreich [Austrian Federal Chamber]. Directory of members; search by company name, place (standort) and product.

Belgium – Sectoral Publications
http://www.abh-ace.be/en/importers/sectoral_publications

> Belgian Foreign Trade Agency. Company directories in eight sector profiles – biotechnology, software, advanced materials, sustainable energy, waste & recycling, food, digital banking and cosmetics.

Bosnia & Herzegovina – Exporters Directory
http://komorabih.ba/en/bhepa/exporters-directory

> Foreign Trade Chamber of Bosnia & Herzegovina. Search by industry category or company name.

Bulgaria Trade Directory
http://www.bcci.bg/services/directory.htm

> Bulgaria Chamber of Commerce & Industry. Search free (register as guest); details of companies require subscription.

Croatian Company Directory
http://www1.biznet.hr/HgkWeb/do/extlogon?lang=en_GB

> Croatian Chamber of Economy. Database of all registered business entities in Croatia, provides contact details, business activity, number of employees, company size, and type of organization.

Cyprus Chamber of Commerce & Industry – Member Directory
http://www.ccci.org.cy

> Cyprus Chamber of Commerce & Industry. Search more than 2500 companies by name, town, product/service, or import/export.

Greater Copenhagen – Fact Sheets [Denmark]
http://www.copcap.com/download

> Greater Copenhagen. Sector profiles include company lists: fintech, pharmaceuticals & biotech, materials, life sciences, smart cities, and green building. (Registration required.)

Estonian Export Directory
http://www.estonianexport.ee/catalogue

> Estonian Chamber of Commerce & Industry. Browse by product/service category, or search by name, location, etc. The Chamber's membership directory of 3000+ companies is at *http://www.koda.ee/en/members*.

Helsinki Region Chamber of Commerce – KauppakamariVerkko [Finland]
https://www.kauppakamariverkko.fi

All 17,000 member companies are listed in the database. Keyword search.

Bottin [France]
http://www.bottin.fr

Teamwork S.P.R.L. Products and services database for France. Search by keyword for company names of products, or under tab "index des rubriques" browse by product category.

SIRENE [France]
https://www.sirene.fr/sirene/public/accueil

INSEE. Sirene (Système informatisé du répertoire des entreprises et des établissements) records all companies and their establishments, whatever their legal form, in any sector, located in France or in the overseas départements. Also listed are foreign companies represented or active in France.

Wer Liefert Was [Germany, Austria, Switzerland]
https://www.wlw.de

Wer Liefert Was? GmbH. "Who supplies what?" supplier database for Germany, Austria and Switzerland. Products and services from 530,000 suppliers, producers, distributors and service providers. Search by 47,000 product/service headings.

Ireland – Sector Profiles and Company Directories
https://www.enterprise-ireland.com/en/Source-a-Product-or-Service-from-Ireland/Sector-and-Company-Directories

Enterprise Ireland. Directories and cluster information for 21 sectors, from aerospace to travel sector solutions.

Athens Chamber of Commerce & Industry – Business Directory [Greece]
http://www.acci.gr/acci/catalogue/search.jsp?context=201

Search 85,000 member companies by keyword, location, business activity, and whether exporting. Search for exporters by name in the **Greek Export Directory** at *http://dir.icap.gr/acci/index.htm*.

Malta – B2B Directory
http://www.maltachamber.org.mt/en/b2b-directory

Malta Chamber of Commerce. Browse by industry sector or search by keyword.

Buy from Portugal
http://export.portugalglobal.pt/export

Portugal Trade & Investment Agency. Keyword search for Portuguese suppliers.

Romanian Exporters Directory
http://www.romania-export.com

Intended for "foreign companies seeking reliable suppliers and partners in Romania," the directory covers manufacturers, importers and exporters. Browse by industry, or search by company name and address.

Major Companies in Romania
http://doingbusiness.ro/upp/MCR2016.pdf

> DoingBusiness.ro. Rankings of companies by industry sector.

ProBusiness Romania
http://www.snia.ro/ContentPages/ProBusiness.aspx

> ProNational Business Information System. Top 50,000 Romanian businesses. ($)

SloExport – Database of Slovenian Exporters
http://www.sloexport.si/en

> Invest Slovenia. Information on more than 4500 Slovenian exporters. Search by companies, trademarks, industry or destination country.

Consultar Censo Nacional de Empresas [Spain]
http://www.camaras.org/censo/consulta.html#

> Spanish Chamber of Commerce – National Census of Businesses. Search by name, address, postal code, and business category.

Export and Import Spanish Companies Directory
http://directory.camaras.org

> Spanish Chamber of Commerce. Search by TARIC code (combination of HS code and local European provisions, e.g. quotas) and country of export/import.

Switzerland – Leading Companies
http://leadingcompanies.s-ge.com

Switzerland Global Enterprise. Search tool for 800+ companies, by location and sector. Uses a geographical display. Click on a displayed company to open a visiting card with details about sales, number of employees, pictures of the company's products, etc.

Companies House [UK]
https://beta.companieshouse.gov.uk

Gov.UK. UK limited companies are incorporated and dissolved through Companies House, which registers company information and makes it available to the public.

1000 Companies to Inspire – Britain
https://www.lseg.com/resources/1000-companies-inspire

London Stock Exchange Group. 1000 of the fastest growing SMEs in the UK. Company profiles grouped by broad categories: creative industries, food & drink, retail, technology & digital, leisure, and green, plus Scottish firms.

ILLUSTRATION: My client Lillian hand paints silk scarves; she has asked me to help her find "a wholesaler" in Paris.

Step 1: In **Section 5a**, Europages directory delivers 52 company names by searching "scarves" and filtering to France; the company type filter shows 22 of these are manufacturers so perhaps are Lillian's competitors, to be studied later. Half the retailers, distributors and wholesalers are in Paris.

In Kompass directory a simple search of "scarves" and "Paris" provides 25 company names. Looking at "activities", 10 of these companies are manufacturers of "neckties, cravats, scarves and shawls" – more local competitors. Among the distributors are a wide variety of different types of company – a few are fashion houses, two are high-end retail stores. There are also differing product ranges – some specialize in men's clothing, some in outerwear, several in accessories.

Step 2: We **consider the options** we've unearthed. Does a distributor need to be in *Paris*? Lillian's scarves could be in other places where people spend money on luxuries – say in retail outlets in airports, art galleries, ski resorts and hotels? Is her real need a *retailer* rather than a distributor – could she work to align her unique product with other one-of-a-kind or high-value products, for example a jewellery or accessories retail chain?

Step 3: What might be the **next step**? With this range of possible distributor types and market positioning, before she contacts any of the companies Lillian could test her options by participating in a trade show (**Section 7b**), a good place to meet potential partners *and* to learn from competitors. Paris Fashion Week and the Accessories Show within ApparelSourcing Paris both happen twice a year for trade visitors such as distributors, rather than the general public. Other resources in this section of the toolbox provide guidance on how to get the most from such a show, and **Section 3c** and **Section 6 Arts & culture** both list programs that provide financial support for such market prospecting.

6. Sector-specific resources

Advanced manufacturing
Aerospace
Agri-food
Arts & cultural products
Automotive & transport
Clean technologies
Construction & infrastructure
Consumer products & services
Forest products
Information & communications technologies
Life sciences
Mining, metals & minerals
Professional services
Public sector procurement

In this section are sector-specific guides, market overviews, regulations, and company directories – valuable resources for finding information about your target market and potential buyers and partners.

If you are selling products or services into a different sector – for example, a software developer targeting the life sciences sector, or a cleantech innovator with potential purchasers in the public-sector agencies in Europe – also investigate the resources relating to your own sector to identify key local competitors. This section also includes sector-specific programs which provide funding and other support for market research and market entry.

Advanced manufacturing

Guides & markets

Plastics Materials & Machinery Export Guide
http://trade.gov/industry/materials (click on Plastics Export Guide)

> US International Trade Administration. Written for US exporters, provides 4- to 5-page country snapshots for European Union and 21 countries including Croatia, Czech Republic, France, Germany, Hungary, Poland, Spain, Sweden, Turkey and the UK. 58 pages, 2015.

Study on the Uptake of Advanced Manufacturing in Europe
http://ec.europa.eu/growth/tools-databases/newsroom/cf/itemdetail.cfm?item_id=9061&lang=en

> European Commission. An analysis of drivers, barriers and readiness factors of EU companies for adopting advanced manufacturing products and technologies. 93 pages, Jan. 2017.

Report on 3D-printing
http://ec.europa.eu/growth/tools-databases/newsroom/cf/itemdetail.cfm?item_id=8937&lang=en

> European Commission. Application areas, industrial value chains and missing competences in the EU. Covers surgical planning, plastic-based car interior components, metallic structural parts for airplanes, inert and hard implants, metal AM for injection molding, spare parts for machines, lighting & other home decoration, 3D-printed textiles, affordable houses, and 3D-printed confectionery. 458 pages, Sept. 2016.

Top Markets Series
http://trade.gov/topmarkets

US International Trade Administration. Written for US exporters, the reports rank future export opportunities within 27 industries including industrial automation, manufacturing technology, and semiconductors & related equipment. Each industry report provides a market assessment of the competitiveness, opportunities and challenges. Case studies on industrial automation in Germany, manufacturing technology in Germany, and semiconductors in the EU.

Exporting Electronics & Electrical Engineering to Europe
https://www.cbi.eu/market-information/electronics-electrical-engineering

Netherlands, Centre for Promotion of Imports. Written for exporters from developing countries, gives tips for finding buyers, channels, and most promising export products.

Regulations & standards

Export Permits for Cryptographic Items
http://www.international.gc.ca/controls-controles/export-exportation/crypto/Crypto_Intro.aspx

Global Affairs Canada. Explains export permit applications for information security goods/technology and goods/technology employing cryptography.

Guidelines for CE Marking on Electro-discharge Machines
http://www.cecimo.eu/site/fileadmin/Publications/CE_Guides /CE_guide_EDM_072015.pdf

> CECIMO. Machinery and equipment must bear CE marking, indicating that the product complies with all relevant requirements of the applicable directive(s). This guide was written for manufacturers, sellers and users of machine tools, and customs authorities, to identify noncompliant products. 24 pages, July 2015.

Companies & organizations

EPTDA Digital Blue Book
http://www.eptda.org/About-EPTDA/BLUE-BOOK-MEMBERS-DIRECTORY/Digital-Blue-Book

> European Power Transmission Distributors Association. Annual directory includes profiles of distributor members, manufacturers, and associate members; and product index.

CECIMO – Members
http://www.cecimo.eu/site/about-us/members

> European Association of the Machine Tool Industries. Links 15 national associations of machine tool builders, most with their own member lists – approximately 1500 industrial enterprises in Europe.

CETOP Directory & Buyers Guide
https://www.cetop.org/directory

> Comité Européen des Transmissions Oléohydrauliques et Pneumatiques. Directory of 1000 companies in the European fluid-power industry, by country. 136 pages, 2017.

EFFRA – Membership
http://www.effra.eu

European Factories of the Future Research Association.
Profiles of corporate, research and association/cluster
members.

EurAi – Member Societies
https://www.eurai.org/organisation/member-societies

European Association for Artificial Intelligence. Links to
artificial intelligence associations in Europe.

EuroMAP Plastics and Rubber Buyers Guide
http://www.euromap.org/buyers-guide

European Plastics & Rubber Machinery. Machinery
manufacturers of Austria, France, Germany, Italy, Spain,
Switzerland, Turkey and the UK. National associations
from other countries listed at
http://www.euromap.org/trade-associations.

Robotics Tomorrow – Company Directory
https://www.roboticstomorrow.com/company_directory_search.php

LJB Management Inc. Online trade magazine covering the
robotics, advanced manufacturing and factory automation
sectors. Search the international company directory by
name, geographic region, and industry sub-sector.

MachineTools.com
https://www.machinetools.com/en/companies/home

MachineWeb, Inc. Worldwide directory of companies and
organizations, by 36 categories. Search by category, then
filter by country. Provides general information, contact
information, and products or services offered, for more
than 32,000 companies. (Registration required.)

Electronic Services Directory
https://www.ventureoutsource.com/contract-manufacturing/search-ems-resources-directory

> VentureOutsource.com. Directory of electronics products and services; search by facilities location, services offered, or target sector.

List of Cluster Organizations
https://www.clustercollaboration.eu/cluster-list

> European Cluster Collaboration Platform. Under "sectoral industries", choose production technology & heavy machinery, or process control; under "emerging industries" choose advanced packaging, or under "technology fields" choose industrial manufacturing, to find links to clusters such as the Mechatronics Cluster in Linz, Austria. Cluster organizations often provide directories of participating companies, universities and other organizations in the sector.

Support for market research & market entry

Early Stage Exporters
http://www.occ.ca/programs/early-stage-exporters

> Ontario Chamber of Commerce. Four categories of activities are funded: direct contacts, marketing tools, market research and foreign bidding projects. Companies must be in a priority sector: advanced manufacturing, aerospace, building products and construction, clean technology, exportable professional services e.g. engineering, ICT, and life sciences.

FedNor – Innovation Fund
http://fednor.gc.ca/eic/site/fednor-
fednor.nsf/eng/fn03444.html

FedNor. Eligible project activities include a) activities related to applied R&D with commercial market potential, including early stage marketing, outreach and promotional initiatives, product, process and service certifications, and market research and technical studies to determine needs and direct future R&D and b) activities that enable organizations and SMEs to increase the level of innovation, productivity, quality and competitiveness in key sectors, including manufacturing.

Advanced manufacturing and aerospace are both technology sectors where innovation is an essential ingredient for export success. Remember to check resources in Section 4b for guidance on protecting your intellectual property (patents, circuit topographies, etc.) in European countries.

Aerospace

Guides & markets

Business with ESA
http://www.esa.int/About_Us/Business_with_ESA

European Space Agency. Industry portal providing information on ESA's Business Opportunities and how to do business with ESA, such as how to prepare good proposals.

Top Markets Series – Aircraft parts
http://trade.gov/topmarkets/aircraft.asp

US International Trade Administration. Written for US exporters, the report ranks future export opportunities in the aircraft parts industry, providing a market assessment of the competitiveness, opportunities and challenges. France, UK, Germany, and Netherlands are in the top 10 markets; the report includes a 2-page profile of the market in Germany.

Aerospace Resource Guide
http://2016.export.gov/industry/aerospace/aerospaceresourcegu ide/index.asp

US Dept. of Commerce. Written for US exporters, this guide provides brief market overviews for 37 countries including Austria, Belgium, Bulgaria, Czech Republic, Denmark, Finland, France, Germany, Hungary, Ireland, Italy, Netherlands, Norway, Poland, Romania, Slovak Republic, Spain, Sweden, Switzerland, Turkey, and the UK. Each country analysis details market entry, current market trends, current demand, barriers, and associations. A subsector reference chart rates US export potential for 14 subsectors in each country. 177 pages, 2015.

Regulations & standards

EASA – Regulations
https://www.easa.europa.eu/regulations

European Aviation Safety Agency. Descriptions and forms for safety regulations such as airworthiness and product certification.

ASD-STAN – Standardization
https://www.asd-stan.org

ASD-STAN is an association which develops standards for the European aerospace industry. Search for and purchase standards from the website.

Companies & organizations

ESA SME Database
http://smed.esa.int

European Space Agency. Search by company name, location and field of experience.

SME4SPACE – Members
https://www.sme4space.org/sme4space-members

SME4SPACE facilitates the access of SMEs to space activities in general and to European Space Agency and EU programs. Links to 14 national member associations.

ASD – Members
http://www.asd-europe.org/about-us/members

AeroSpace and Defence Industries Association of Europe. Links to 26 national associations.

List of Cluster Organizations
https://www.clustercollaboration.eu/cluster-list

European Cluster Collaboration Platform. Under "sectoral industries", choose aerospace vehicles and defense, or under "technology fields" choose aerospace technology, to find links to clusters such as the Hamburg Aviation e.V. cluster in Germany. Cluster organizations often provide directories of participating companies, universities and other organizations in the sector.

Support for market research & market entry

Early Stage Exporters
http://www.occ.ca/programs/early-stage-exporters

Ontario Chamber of Commerce. Four categories of activities are funded: direct contacts, marketing tools, market research and foreign bidding projects. Companies must be in a priority sector: advanced manufacturing, aerospace, building products, clean technology, exportable professional services such as engineering, ICT, or life sciences.

Agri-food

Guides & markets

Following the Road Signals of Export-Readiness
http://www5.agr.gc.ca/resources/prod/Internet-Internet/MISB-DGSIM/ATS-SEA/PDF/4330-eng.pdf

> Agriculture and Agri-Food Canada. Identify your first priorities; More detailed preparatory measures; Evaluate your export preparedness. Chapters include your company, your product, export preparation, market entry and distribution, pricing, and promotion. 17 pages.

Doing Business in Europe
http://www.agr.gc.ca/eng/industry-markets-and-trade/foreign-market-information-by-region/?id=1410083148447 (click on Europe)

> Agriculture & Agri-Food Canada. This page brings together market intelligence, regulatory requirements, CETA, trade data and analysis, and agri-food and seafood news.

Canadian Opportunities in the European Union
http://www.agr.gc.ca/eng/?id=1491417397651

> Agriculture & Agri-Food Canada. Identifies the largest and fastest-growing opportunities for agri-food products, specific opportunities and their top three EU markets, the top 3 supplying provinces, plus a summary of non-EU competitors to Canada in the EU market. 2016.

Emerging Food Innovation: Trends & Opportunities
*http://www.agr.gc.ca/resources/prod/doc/pdf/emerging_food_*
innovations_innovations_alimentaires_emergentes-eng.pdf

> Agriculture & Agri-Food Canada. Summary of current trends and emerging opportunities for innovation available to the food processing industry. Covers consumer preferences, marketplace pressures, innovative ingredients, and emerging technologies. 9 pages, Nov. 2015.

Global Food and Drink Trends 2017
http://www.mintel.com/global-food-and-drink-trends-2016

> Mintel. Trends include interest in traditional products & styles, expansion of vegetarian and other plant-focused formulations, quick fix products and meals, and healthy products. 22 pages. (Registration required.)

Food Retail Online in Germany
http://www.ey.com/Publication/vsLUAssets/EY-report-food-
online-germany/$File/EY-report-food-online-germany.pdf

> EY. One in six Germans shops for food online, especially top earners and urban dwellers. 21 pages, May 2017 (in German).

An Overview of e-Commerce Trends in the UK
http://www.agr.gc.ca/resources/prod/Internet-Internet/MISB-
DGSIM/ATS-SEA/PDF/6803-eng.pdf

> Agriculture & Agri-Food Canada. Consumer spending online; grocery marketplace trends. 2 pages, 2016.

Statistics and Market Information
http://www.agr.gc.ca/eng/industry-markets-and-trade/statistics-and-market-information/?id=1361289956531

Agriculture and Agri-Food Canada. Brief overview reports of the market for food and beverage products in foreign markets. Market reports are organized by product or country.

Global Agricultural Information Network (GAIN)
http://gain.fas.usda.gov/Lists/Advanced%20Search/AllItems.aspx

US Department of Agriculture, Foreign Agricultural Service. Information on the agricultural situation in more than 130 countries, issued as reports such as Taiwan Pet Food Market, Japan Food Trends, UK Organic Products Market Report, etc. Search options include date and categories/countries/posts. (Registration required.)

Regulations & standards

Food Exports
http://www.inspection.gc.ca (under Food tab, click Exports)

Canadian Food Inspection Agency. CFIA verifies that exported food and food products meet Canadian requirements (where applicable) as well as those of the importing country. This page provides information on exporting dairy products, eggs and egg products, fish and seafood, foods regulated solely under the Food and Drugs Act and Regulations, fresh fruits and vegetables, honey, meat and poultry products, and processed products (fruits, vegetables and maple products), as well as other foods manufactured in Canada.

Agricultural Market Access Database
https://www.oecd.org/site/amad

> OECD. Data includes bound tariff quota volumes, in- and over-quota tariff rates, MFN tariff rates, TRQ country allocations, and import volume and value. (Registration required.)

DOOR – Database of Origin and Registration
http://ec.europa.eu/agriculture/quality/door/list.html

> European Commission. List of more than 1500 trademarks and designs on agricultural and food products, registered or applied for under three EU quality and name protection schemes: PDO – protected designation of origin, PGI – protected geographical indication, and TSG – traditional speciality guaranteed.

EU Guidance Document... Import Requirements [food safety]
https://ec.europa.eu/food/safety/international_affairs/trade/index_en.htm

> European Commission. This Guidance document is sub-titled "Key questions related to import requirements and the EU rules on food hygiene and official food controls." Provides a general framework for official controls performed by the EU Member States to verify compliance with feed and food law, animal health and animal welfare.

FreshQuality – Your Guide to EU Fresh Produce Law
http://www.freshquality.eu/php/home.php

> European Fresh Produce Association. Sections of the website cover food safely, labelling & nutrition, hygiene, quality standards, packaging, and other legislation.

Global Organic Trade Guide
http://www.globalorganictrade.com/country-list

Written for US exporters, includes short reports on
Western Europe and Scandinavia, and for each country
with organic regulations, and indication of whether these
are voluntary or enforced. Under Import Information, find
links to regulations in European Union, Switzerland and
Ukraine.

A Pocket Guide to the EU's New Fish and Aquaculture Consumer Labels
https://ec.europa.eu/fisheries/pocket-guide-eus-new-fish-and-aquaculture-consumer-labels_en

European Commission. This guide explains what must
appear on labels and what additional information can be
displayed. 20 pages, 2014.

Food Labelling and Packaging [UK]
https://www.gov.uk/food-labelling-and-packaging/overview

GOV.UK. Contents include overview, food labelling,
ingredients list, food & drink warnings, nutrition, health
claims & supplement labelling, and organic food.

Food Supplement Regulations Guide
http://www.lexmundi.com/lexmundi/Food_Supplement_Regulations_Guide.asp

Lex Mundi. Information necessary to estimate the
possibility of selling a given product on a market and the
time and cost related to administrative procedures and
preparation of labelling. Countries covered include
Austria, Cyprus, Czech Republic, Estonia, Finland, Greece,
Hungary, Ireland, Latvia, Lithuania, Norway, Poland,
Portugal, Romania, Slovenia, Sweden, and Switzerland.
80 pages, 2012.

Registering Plant Protection Products in the EU
http://www.ecpa.eu/sites/default/files/7450_Registration%20
brochure_3.pdf

> European Crop Protection. Overview of EU legislation, tests & studies required for plant protection products, and how the approval process works. 20 pages, 2013.

Agribusiness Guide
http://www.lexmundi.com/lexmundi/Agribusiness_Guide.asp

> Lex Mundi. Requirements to sell, manufacture or commercialize transgenics, insecticides, pesticides, herbicides and rodenticides. Countries covered include Cyprus, Ireland, Netherlands and Spain. 37 pages, 2013.

Companies & organizations

European Spice Association – Members
https://www.esa-spices.org/index-esa.html/members-esa

> European Spice Association. Directory of 13 national associations and 60+ member companies in Europe.

IADSA – Member Associations
http://www.iadsa.org

> International Alliance of Dietary/Food Supplement Associations. Contact information for member associations in Bulgaria, Czech Republic, Denmark, Finland, Germany, Italy, Romania, Serbia, Spain, Turkey, the UK and for Food Supplements Europe.

FoodDrinkEurope – Members
http://www.fooddrinkeurope.eu

FoodDrinkEurope. FoodDrinkEurope is an alliance of food industry associations; sectors include associations such as FEDIAF – European Pet Food Industry Federation; national federations include associations such as the Finnish Food and Drink Industries' Federation – Elintarviketeollisuusliitto.

List of Cluster Organizations
https://www.clustercollaboration.eu/cluster-list

European Cluster Collaboration Platform. Under "sectoral industries", choose food processing; or under "technology fields" choose agriculture or agrofood industry, to find links to clusters such as the Asociación Clúster Alimentario de Galicia cluster in Santiago de Compostela, Spain. Cluster organizations often provide directories of participating companies, universities and other organizations in the sector.

Support for market research & market entry

Single Window Contact for Agri-Food Trade Services
http://www.agr.gc.ca/eng/?id=1458757288711

Agriculture & Agri-Food Canada. This service offers a single point of contact to help the Canadian food industry and businesses reach international markets. Find the markets with the most potential for your business; promote your products at key international trade shows; use the Canada Brand program to market your food products.

Canadian Food Exporters Association
https://www.cfea.com/benefits

Canadian Food Exporters Association. For association members, CFEA will do market-specific searches. CFEA also organizes a number of trade shows per year (retail, foodservice, and specialty & private label) – members benefit from reduced pricing on space, shipping, and travel, as well as saving staff time. ($)

Canadian Vintners Association – Funding Opportunities
http://www.canadianvintners.com/initiatives/funding-opportunities

Canadian Vintners Association. Through its Agri-Marketing Program, the federal government provides funding to the Association to assist wineries with travel expenses to domestic and international wine fairs, tastings and festivals. One representative per winery is eligible to apply for financial assistance with travel expenses.

FedNor – Innovation Fund
http://fednor.gc.ca/eic/site/fednor-fednor.nsf/eng/fn03444.html

FedNor. Eligible project activities include a) activities related to applied R&D with commercial market potential, including early stage marketing, outreach and promotional initiatives, product, process and service certifications, and market research and technical studies to determine needs and direct future R&D and b) activities that enable organizations and SMEs to increase the level of innovation, productivity, quality and competitiveness in key sectors, including agri-food.

Arts & cultural products

Guides & markets

The Art of Export Marketing
http://www.culturalhrc.ca/em/index-e.php

Cultural Human Resources Council. Provides information to help artists and cultural workers understand the skills needed to export their work to international markets; guides them with a list of tools and websites for essential exporting information.

Export Readiness
http://www.workinculture.ca/Resources/Export-Readiness

WorkInCulture & Craft Ontario. Video tips and resources help artists and craftspeople export their work internationally. Topics include networking internationally, researching markets, online sales, shipping, policies and pricing, and working with customs.

International Digital Media Co-Production Guide for Canadian Companies
https://trends.cmf-fmc.ca/research-reports/international-digital-media-co-production-guide-for-canadian-companies

Interactive Ontario. Gives local interactive digital media and cross-platform producers a better understanding of international digital media co-production. Detailed Country Information section covers where to start looking for partners, what funding might be available and what issues there might be with a co-production in countries including France, Germany and the UK. 57 pages, 2014

Exporting Jewellery to Europe
https://www.cbi.eu/market-information/jewellery

> Netherlands, Centre for the Promotion of Imports. Written for exporters from developing countries. Gives tips for finding buyers, channels, and most promising export products.

Top Markets Series – Media & Entertainment
http://trade.gov/topmarkets

> US International Trade Administration. The media and entertainment report reviews seven global licensing and export markets and two regions across four broad sectors: book publishing, filmed entertainment, music, and video games. Highlighted countries include Germany, Nordic countries and the UK. Includes sector snapshots on each sector.

Discoverability: Strategies for Canada's Digital Content Producers...
http://cmpa.ca/sites/default/files/documents/industry-information/studies/CMPA%20DISCOVERABILITY%20STUDY.pdf

> Canadian Media Production Association. Examples of successful digital marketing campaigns and strategies to improve "discoverability" in a global marketplace in which apps, games and videos compete with film and TV products. Covers size of the global marketplace, discoverability trends including a checklist, case studies, and digital awards and events. 42 pages, 2013. A database of digital content conferences and tradeshows, **Digital Events Advisor**, is at *www.digitaleventsadvisor.com*.

World Cities Culture Finance Report
*http://www.worldcitiescultureforum.com/assets/others/170516_
WCCF_FullReport.pdf*

World Cities Culture Forum. Includes detailed profiles of
the cultural funding landscape in 16 cities including
Amsterdam, Brussels, Istanbul, London, Paris, Stockholm
and Toronto.

**Music Market in Germany and Opportunities for Canadian
Companies**
http://researchlibrary.omdc.on.ca

Canadian Association for the Advancement of Music and
the Arts. Intended to provide Canadian music industry
companies with market intelligence about Germany and
to stimulate export activity. Germany is the premier
market in Europe and is an access point for the European
marketplace. 39 pages, April 2014.

Music Consumer Insight Report 2016
*http://www.ifpi.org/downloads/Music-Consumer-Insight-
Report-2016.pdf*

Ispos Connect for IFPI. The behaviour of music consumers
across 13 of the world's major music markets, with new
information on changing consumer behaviours. Markets
examined include Great Britain, France, Germany, Spain,
Italy, and Sweden. 20 pages, 2016.

Ireland Music Market Report
http://www.caama.org/wp-content/uploads/Ireland-Report-2016-4-6-2016.pdf

> Canadian Association for the Advancement of Music and the Arts. Overview of the state of the music market, detailed information about local record labels, distributors, booking agencies, media and other promotional contacts, venues and festivals, and best practices for touring in the market. 36 pages, April 2016.

UK Music Market Report
http://www.omdc.on.ca/Assets/Research/Research+Reports/CAAMA+-UK+Report+2016/CAAMA+-+UK+Report+2016.pdf

> Canadian Association for the Advancement of Music and the Arts. Overview of the state of the music market, detailed information about local record labels, distributors, booking agencies, media and other promotional contacts, venues and festivals, and best practices for touring in the market. 58 pages, April 2016.

Creative Economy Outlook and Country Profiles
http://unctad.org/en/PublicationsLibrary/webditcted2016d5_en.pdf

> UN Conference on Trade & Development. Trade performance of developing and developed countries in key creative industries sectors such as design, music, film, TV, broadcasting, books, arts & crafts and new media. Includes 2-page statistical profiles for Austria, Belgium, Bulgaria, Cyprus, Denmark, Estonia, Finland, France, Germany, Hungary, Iceland, Ireland, Latvia, Lithuania, Luxembourg, Malta, Norway, Poland, Portugal, Romania, Slovakia, Slovenia, Spain, Sweden, Switzerland, Netherlands, Turkey and the UK. 169 pages, July 2016.

The New Faces of Gaming
http://www.isfe.eu/industry-facts/statistics

Interactive Software Federation of Europe. There is a growing appetite for gaming across a whole range of age and gender groups. 5 pages, Feb. 2017.

Regulations & standards

Services Trade Restrictiveness Index
http://www.oecd.org/tad/services-trade/services-trade-restrictiveness-index.htm

OECD. Country Notes are 2-page analytical summaries of policies that restrict services trade for 44 countries. Sector Notes describe restrictions in 18 sectors including motion picture, sound recording, and television and broadcasting. The Regulatory Database covers specific laws and regulations that contribute to services trade restrictiveness – filter by sector and country.

SME Guides and Manuals
http://www.wipo.int/sme/en/documents/guides

World Intellectual Property Organization. A series of guides for small business, including "Creative expression: An introduction to copyright" and "Marketing crafts and visual arts: The role of intellectual property".

Managing Intellectual Property in the Book Publishing Industry
http://www.wipo.int/edocs/pubdocs/en/copyright/868/wipo_pub_868.pdf

World Intellectual Property Organization. This introductory guide offers practical information to help book publishers exploit their own IP rights as economic assets and to avoid infringing on the IP rights of others. 86 pages, 2007.

Rights, Camera, Action! IP rights and the film-making process
http://www.wipo.int/publications/en/details.jsp?id=256&plang=EN

World Intellectual Property Organization. Written for independent film-makers from developing countries, this guide provides an accessible introduction to some essential intellectual property issues. 98 pages, 2007.

From Script to Screen: The importance of copyright in the distribution of films
http://www.wipo.int/publications/en/details.jsp?id=261&plang=EN

World Intellectual Property Organization. Written for novice film-makers, this guide introduces the principles and standards of the international movie industry and identifies some key legal and business issues. 149 pages, 2011.

Global VAT Guide – Cross-border supplies of intangible services, rights and digital content
https://www.dlapiper.com/~/media/Files/Insights/Publications/2016/05/Global_VAT_Guide_2016.pdf

DLA Piper. OECD VAT guidelines, tips for minimizing VAT (GST) risks for cross-border supplies, and sections on Finland, France, Germany, Italy, Luxembourg, Netherlands, Norway, Poland, Russia, Spain, Sweden, and the UK. 56 pages, May 2016.

Taxation of Artists in an International Context
http://www.pearle.ws/_cms/files/file_sys_Publications_Bijlage_Engels_51.pdf

European Festivals Association & Pearle Live Performance Europe. Part of the series The Ultimate Cookbook for Cultural Managers. International taxation rules for artists, touring companies, festivals and other players. 46 pages, March 2016.

VAT in an International Context
*http://www.pearle.ws/_cms/files/file_sys_Publications_Bijlage_
Engels_52.pdf*

> European Festivals Association & Pearle Live Performance
> Europe. Part of the series The Ultimate Cookbook for
> Cultural Managers. This brochure explains the
> consequences of VAT in an international context and what
> you must do to comply with the European rules. 40 pages,
> Jan. 2017.

Companies & organizations

AEAA – Members
http://www.aeaa.info

> European Association of Artist Managers. Find more than
> 70 artist managers, concert agents and impresarios from
> 17 countries.

CMA – Who Represents Whom
http://www.classicalmusicartists.com

> Classical Music Artists. Find more than 150 music artists'
> agents in 16 European countries.

FEAGA – Members
http://www.europeangalleries.org/?page_id=2

> Federation of European Art Galleries Association. List of
> art gallery associations whose websites contain lists of art
> galleries.

EFFE – Europe for Festivals, Festivals for Europe
http://www.effe.eu

European Festivals Association. Database of more than 700 festivals in 39 countries. Covers architecture, circus, dance, design, digital arts, film, heritage, literature, music, opera, photography, spoken word, storytelling, street arts, theatre and visual arts. Search by keyword, date, country and genre.

List of Cluster Organizations
https://www.clustercollaboration.eu/cluster-list

European Cluster Collaboration Platform. Under "sectoral industries", choose jewelry, music, performing arts or video production; under "technology fields" choose multimedia or creative products & services; or under "emerging industries" choose creative industries, to find links to clusters such as the Transylvania Textile & Fashion Cluster in Sfantu Gheorghe, Romania. Cluster organizations often provide directories of participating companies, universities and other organizations in the sector.

Support for market research & market entry

Overview of Existing Canadian Export Support Programs
https://trends.cmf-fmc.ca/research-reports/overview-of-existing-canadian-export-support-programs

Canada Media Fund. 25 Canadian export support programs of national and regional scope offer promotional and marketing activities for Canadian media productions, including business trips, participation in trade fairs and missions, technology development, the hiring of consultants and the development of business expansion strategies. 10 pages, Dec. 2016.

Arts Abroad
http://canadacouncil.ca/funding/grants/arts-abroad

Canada Council for the Arts. Program components are travel, representation and promotion, translation, circulation and touring, residencies, and co-productions.

IDM Fund: Global Market Development
http://www.omdc.on.ca/interactive/Interactive_Digital_Media_F und/Global_Market_Development.htm

Ontario Media Development Corporation. Provides eligible Ontario companies with funding to participate in international activities that support company growth and produce measurable business and market development results. Primary activities supported include targeted sales trips and attendance at international market events.

FACTOR: Foundation Assisting Canadian Talent on Recordings
http://www.factor.ca/our-programs/our-programs-overview

The Artist Development Program subsidizes development activities such as recording, touring, video production and marketing. The Live Performance program subsidizes the cost of international performances including showcases and tours. Support for Eligible Music Companies provides funding for business development initiatives that support the marketing and promotion of the company, and international business travel.

Telefilm Canada: Export Assistance Program
https://telefilm.ca/en/financing/export

Telefilm Canada. Support for foreign companies acquiring Canadian films, with the objective of increasing the visibility of Canadian talent and productions internationally. A pilot program for fiscal 2016–2017.

International Marketing and Festival Participation Program
https://telefilm.ca/en/financing/international-marketing-festival-participation

Telefilm Canada. Helps Canadian production companies finance the promotion and international marketing of their productions that have been officially selected at an international festival; producers are invited to an international co-production forum.

Automotive & transport

Guides & markets

Exporting Automotive Parts and Components to Europe
https://www.cbi.eu/market-information/automotive-parts-components

Netherlands Ministry of Foreign Affairs. Written for developing countries. Answers market research questions such as What requirements should my product comply with? What competition do I face? How do I find buyers?

Automobile Industry Pocket Guide
http://www.acea.be/uploads/publications/ACEA_Pocket_Guide_2017-2018.pdf

European Automobile Manufacturers' Association. Tables and statistics about the EU and global auto industries, such as vehicle production, registration, use and taxation. Also includes the latest figures on employment and trade, innovation, and environmental performance. 78 pages.

Returning to Growth: A Look at the European Automotive Aftermarket
http://www.acea.be/uploads/publications/BCG_Returning_to_Growth_Jul_2014.pdf

European Automobile Manufacturers' Association & Boston Consulting Group. A brief overview of competition and trends in the automotive repair market. 18 pages, 2014.

European Alternative Fuels Observatory
http://www.eafo.eu

The European Commission initiative provides alternative fuels statistics and information – electricity, hydrogen, natural gas, and LPG. Also includes country statistics, city procurement goals, incentives and legislation.

Global Electric Vehicle Outlook 2017
http://www.iea.org/publications/freepublications/publication/ GlobalEVOutlook2017.pdf

International Energy Agency. This report mainly covers the electric car market and other transport modes in less detail. Countries include Canada, Iceland, India, Liechtenstein, Norway, Switzerland, Turkey, and each of the member countries of the European Union (EU 28). 71 pages, 2017.

Overview on Tax Incentives for Electric Vehicles
http://www.acea.be/uploads/publications/EV_incentives_overvie w_2017.pdf

European Automobile Manufacturers' Association. Brief description of incentives, by country.

EMTA Barometer
http://www.emta.com/spip.php?article267

European Metropolitan Transport Authorities. Includes public transport statistics such as car ownership rates, urban density and transport modes, public transport demand trends, and operational costs. 36 pages, 2017.

Directory of Public Transport in European Metropolitan Areas
http://www.emta.com/spip.php?article268

European Metropolitan Transport Authorities. For 28 metropolitan areas, from Amsterdam to Warsaw, provides brief description of governance and operators, public transit systems, and supply/demand statistics (passenger kilometers, fare structures, etc.). 140 pages, 2013.

Top Markets Series
http://trade.gov/topmarkets

US International Trade Administration. Written for US exporters, the reports rank future export opportunities. The automotive parts report includes rankings for original equipment and after-market in 10 European countries and a 4-page profile of the market in Germany. The recreational transport report includes market rankings for recreational marine products, recreational vehicles, miscellaneous vehicles, and motorcycles and parts, and a 6-page profile of the Western Europe market.

Regulations & standards

Motor Vehicles – Approval Authorities in Member States
http://ec.europa.eu/docsroom/documents/24201

European Commission. Contact information including links for agencies responsible for the approval of a type of vehicle, system, component or separate technical unit, or of the individual approval of a vehicle. They issue and withdraw approval certificates.

*Comparative Study on the Differences Between EU and US
Legislation on Emissions in the Automotive Sector*
*http://www.europarl.europa.eu/RegData/etudes/STUD/2016/
587331/IPOL_STU(2016)587331_EN.pdf*

European Parliament. A comparative study on the
differences between the EU and US legislation on
emissions in the automotive sector, covering the
emissions standards themselves; the systems for their
implementation and enforcement, including approval
systems for vehicles; and the respective regimes for
prohibiting the use of defeat devices. 100 pages, 2016.

Companies & organizations

Automotive-Index
http://www.automotive-index.com

Bayern Innovativ GmbH. Database of 4500 suppliers,
research organizations, and associations. Keyword search
or browse by category or country.

List of Cluster Organizations
https://www.clustercollaboration.eu/cluster-list

European Cluster Collaboration Platform. Under "sectoral
industries", choose automotive to find links to clusters
such as the E-Mobility Cluster in Regensburg, Germany.
Cluster organizations often provide directories of
participating companies, universities and other
organizations in the sector.

Clean technologies

Guides & markets

Best Practices of Canadian Engineering and Architectural Firms
http://www.ic.gc.ca/eic/site/si-is.nsf/eng/ai02291.html

Innovation, Science & Economic Development Canada.
Key impediments to business, success factors and best
practices. Though Europe is generally considered a
saturated market, opportunities exist in niche markets,
e.g. clean technologies and environmentally sustainable
projects, given heightened environmental concerns in
many European countries. See especially section 3.2
Strategies to Work Internationally. 48 pages, 2013.

Circular Economy Industry Platform
http://www.circulary.eu

Business Europe. Examples of innovative ways in which
industry, SMEs and other businesses add to the circular
economy in Europe, and regulatory and non-regulatory
challenges these businesses face to upscale their current
initiatives or to start new ones. Linked to a "timeline"
page which presents the state of upcoming legislation.
Country-specific initiatives are identified under Countries
and also in About Us – Resources.

Energy Policies of IEA Countries
https://www.iea.org/publications/countryreviews

International Energy Agency. A report on each country
covers energy policy, such as climate change and energy
efficiency; sector analyses including sector structure, supply
& demand, and participating institutions; and energy
technology research, development and demonstration.
Recent reports for Belgium, Czech Republic, France,
Hungary, Italy, Norway, Poland, and Turkey.

Global Renewable Energy Database
https://www.iea.org/policiesandmeasures/renewableenergy

International Energy Agency. IEA/IRENA joint policies and measures database. Search by country, energy policy target such as solar thermal, and by sector such as heating & cooling, or by keyword.

Prevention of Hazardous Waste in Europe – Status in 2015
https://www.eea.europa.eu/publications/waste-prevention-in-europe

European Environment Agency. Chapters include trends and sources of hazardous waste, prevention of hazardous waste, and country profiles for Austria, Bulgaria, Estonia, France, Germany, Ireland, Latvia, Netherlands, Portugal, Spain, Sweden & the UK. 84 pages, 2016

Green Building Services
https://www.usitc.gov/publications/332/journals/vol_iii_article3_green_building_services.pdf

US International Trade Commission. Overview of the US and global markets for green building services; selected markets include Germany, Norway and the UK. Discusses factors that affect supply and demand for sustainable structures; examines trade in green building services as a component of overall trade in construction, architectural, and engineering services; and considers the outlook for the green building industry. 21 pages, Oct. 2015.

Promoting sustainable building materials and the implications on the use of wood in buildings
https://www.unece.org/fileadmin/DAM/timber/publications/SP-38.pdf

UN Economic Commission for Europe and FAO. Profiles policies and programs from Austria, Germany, Switzerland, Netherlands, and the UK, among others. 124 pages, Sept. 2016.

Buying green! A handbook on green public procurement
*https://publications.europa.eu/en/publication-detail/-
/publication/8c2da441-f63c-11e5-8529-01aa75ed71a1*

> European Commission. Written for public authorities
> planning green public procurement. The handbook follows
> the structure of a procurement procedure, and gives real
> examples of green purchasing by public authorities across
> the EU. It should help suppliers and service providers,
> particularly SMEs, to understand the environmental
> requirements encountered in public tenders. 80 pages, 2016.

Global Market Outlook for Solar Power 2017–2021
*http://www.solarpowereurope.org/reports/global-market-
outlook-2017*

> SolarPower Europe. Sections include trends, European
> solar market segmentation and prospects, and solar in the
> European electricity system. 60 pages, 2017.

About Wind
https://windeurope.org/about-wind

> Wind Europe. European and global statistics and market and
> investment reports, such as Wind Energy Scenarios for 2030.

Battery Energy Storage in the EU
*https://eurobat.org/sites/default/files/eurobat_batteryenergy
storage_web_0.pdf*

> EuroBat. Sections include the EU battery industry and
> market trends and legislative barriers and opportunities in
> Europe. 36 pages, 2016.

Top Markets Series
http://trade.gov/topmarkets

US International Trade Administration. Written for US exporters, the reports rank future export opportunities within 27 industries including building products and sustainable construction, environmental technologies, renewable energy, renewable fuels, and smart grid. Each industry report provides a market assessment of the competitiveness, opportunities and challenges within a sector. Country case studies are included for environmental technologies in Poland, renewable fuels in the EU, and smart grid in Turkey & the UK.

Environmental Technologies Resource Guide
http://2016.export.gov/industry/environment/environmental technologyresourceguide/index.asp

US Commercial Service. Written for US exporters, this guide describes best prospects in the environmental technologies sector: water & wastewater, waste management, air pollution control, and soil remediation. Separate reports for European markets: Czech Republic, Finland, France, Germany, Hungary, Netherlands, Poland, Portugal, Romania, Slovakia and Sweden. Information on trade events, government agencies, and associations. June 2016.

Regulations & standards

More from Less — Material Resource Efficiency in Europe
https://www.eea.europa.eu/publications/more-from-less

European Environment Agency. Resource efficiency and circular economy in Europe – similarities and differences in national policy objectives, priority sectors, driving forces, targets, etc. 60 examples of countries' policy initiatives, described in 32 country profiles.

Smart Grid Standards Map
http://smartgridstandardsmap.com

International Electrotechnical Commission. Includes both relationships between components of the smart grid and standards. In Mapping View, use the Components/Cluster view to find a drop-down list of standards that apply to a component within a functional cluster; use Standards View to start with a known standard and find the other parts of the grid where it applies.

Companies & organizations

SolarPower Europe – Members' Directory
http://www.solarpowereurope.org/membership/list-of-members

SolarPower Europe. Browse by company name or search by keyword, country or category, from equipment to utilities.

Biogas: Companies Catalogue
http://european-biogas.eu/wp-content/uploads/2016/06/Companies-Catalogue-2016-web.pdf

European Biogas Association. Members' directory includes manufacturing, planning, operators, consulting, science & research, and training. 44 pages, Jan. 2016.

List of Cluster Organizations
https://www.clustercollaboration.eu/cluster-list

European Cluster Collaboration Platform. Under "sectoral industries", choose environmental services; under "technology fields" choose energy, transport, waste management, water management, or protecting man and environment; or under "emerging industries" choose environmental industries, to find links to clusters such as the Centre for Energy Technologie Cluster–Free Enterprise Association in Świdnica, Poland. Cluster organizations often provide directories of participating companies, universities and other organizations in the sector.

Support for market research & market entry

Early Stage Exporters
http://www.occ.ca/programs/early-stage-exporters

Ontario Chamber of Commerce. Four categories of activities are funded: direct contacts, marketing tools, market research and foreign bidding projects. Companies must be in a priority sector: Advanced manufacturing; Aerospace; Building products and construction; Clean technology (including renewable energy and environmental technologies); Exportable professional services (e.g., architecture, engineering, urban planning); ICT; or Life sciences.

WaterTAP – Market Insight Program
http://watertapontario.com/bluetech-research-market-insight-program

WaterTAP. The program subsidizes market intelligence reports from BlueTech Research, providing detailed insight and analysis including key market trends, market size and competitive analysis, on markets for water and wastewater technologies and services.

FedNor – Innovation Fund
http://fednor.gc.ca/eic/site/fednor-fednor.nsf/eng/fn03444.html

FedNor. Eligible project activities include a) activities related to applied R&D with commercial market potential, including early stage marketing, outreach and promotional initiatives, product, process and service certifications, and market research and technical studies to determine needs and direct future R&D and b) activities that enable organizations and SMEs to increase the level of innovation, productivity, quality and competitiveness in key sectors, including renewable energy.

Construction & infrastructure

Guides & markets

Top Markets Series
http://trade.gov/topmarkets

> US International Trade Administration. Written for US exporters, the reports rank future export opportunities within 27 industries including building products and sustainable construction, construction equipment, and smart grid. Each industry report provides a market assessment of the competitiveness, opportunities and challenges within a sector. Case studies include building products in the UK and smart grid in Turkey & the UK.

Green Building Services
https://www.usitc.gov/publications/332/journals/vol_iii_articl e3_green_building_services.pdf

> US International Trade Commission. This paper provides an overview of the US and global markets for green building services; selected markets include Germany, Norway and the UK. Discusses factors that affect supply and demand for sustainable structures; examines trade in green building services as a component of overall trade in construction, architectural, and engineering services; and considers the outlook for the green building industry. 21 pages, Oct. 2015.

Promoting Sustainable Building Materials
https://www.unece.org/fileadmin/DAM/timber/publications/SP-38.pdf

> UN Economic Commission for Europe and FAO. Profiles policies and programs from Austria, Germany, Switzerland, Netherlands and the UK, among others. 124 pages, Sept. 2016.

Model Forms [engineering]
http://www.orgalime.org/page/model-forms

European Engineering Industries Association. The association represents the mechanical, electrical & electronic, and metalworking & metal articles industries. Provides model forms for international technology license agreements, exclusive distributor and sales agent contracts, consortium agreements, contracts for technical work on-site, non-disclosure agreements, OEM contracts, and turnkey contracts.

Regulations & standards

Construction Products Regulation
http://ec.europa.eu/growth/sectors/construction/product-regulation_en

European Commission. Home page for information about the Regulation (EU) No. 305/2011, Eurocodes, and support tools to help manufacturers identify key legislation, regulations and standards. EN Eurocodes home page is *http://eurocodes.jrc.ec.europa.eu.*

Outcomes of the Survey on Building Standards and Building Regulations in the UNECE Region
https://www.unece.org/fileadmin/DAM/hlm/documents/Publications/Building_standards_survey_outcomes.pdf

UN Economic Commission for Europe. Survey results describe the building standards and regulations in UNECE countries (Europe and North America) and the challenges the building sector faces; identifies priority areas as thermal performance of buildings and building components. 25 pages, Nov. 2015.

Your Guide to Global Construction and Engineering Law
http://www.eversheds.com/global/en/what/publications/books
.page

> Eversheds. Coverage includes Austria, Belgium, Czech Republic, England & Wales, Estonia, France, Germany, Hungary, Ireland, Italy, Latvia, Lithuania, Netherlands, Poland, Romania, Russia, Scotland, Slovakia, Spain, Sweden and Switzerland. 93 pages, 2014.

Services Trade Restrictiveness Index
http://www.oecd.org/tad/services-trade/services-trade-
restrictiveness-index.htm

> OECD. The Index helps identify which policy measures restrict trade. Country notes offer a 2-page analytical summary of services trade restrictiveness in 44 countries, mainly in Europe. Sector Notes provide an analysis of the 18 different services sectors including architecture, construction, and engineering. The Regulatory Database covers specific laws and regulations that contribute to services trade restrictiveness – filter by sector and country.

Administrative Formalities and Costs Involved in Accessing
Markets Cross-border for Provision of Accountancy, Engineering
and Architecture Services
http://publications.europa.eu/en/publication-detail/-
/publication/5c8a6c62-44e3-11e7-aea8-01aa75ed71a1

> European Commission. Separate sections for accountancy, engineering and architecture describe types of procedures, regulatory requirements, deadlines, fees, etc. 217 pages, May 2017.

Companies & organizations

Construction Products Europe – Our Members
https://www.construction-products.eu/our-members/our-members.aspx

Construction Products Europe. The members of Construction Products Europe are national and European construction products associations. This page provides contact information for the members, whose websites often include directories of member companies.

List of Cluster Organizations
https://www.clustercollaboration.eu/cluster-list

European Cluster Collaboration Platform. Under "sectoral industries", choose construction, or under "technology fields" choose construction technology or transport infrastructure, to find links to clusters such as the Cluster Construcción Sostenible in Tenerife, Spain. Cluster organizations often provide directories of participating companies, universities and other organizations in the sector.

Support for market research & market entry

Early Stage Exporters
http://www.occ.ca/programs/early-stage-exporters

Ontario Chamber of Commerce. Four categories of activities are funded: direct contacts, marketing tools, market research and foreign bidding projects. Companies must be in a priority sector: Advanced manufacturing; Aerospace; Building products and construction; Clean technology; Exportable professional services (e.g., architecture, engineering, urban planning); ICT; or Life sciences.

Expanding Market Opportunities Program
http://www.nrcan.gc.ca/forests/federal-programs/13133

Natural Resources Canada. Two components: Offshore Markets and North America; Natural Resources Canada provides up to 50% of eligible project costs. Eligible recipients under EMO include not-for-profit forest products associations, manufactured housing associations and not-for-profit organizations engaged in forest product research.

For both clean technologies and the construction & infrastructure sectors, local government and public utilities are major customer segments. Check the public sector procurement subsection of **Sector 6**.

Consumer products & services

Markets

Urban World: Global Consumers to Watch
http://www.mckinsey.com/global-themes/urbanization/urban-world-the-global-consumers-to-watch

> McKinsey Global Institute. Nine groups of urban consumers are projected to generate three-quarters of global urban consumption growth from 2015 to 2030. Ranked first are the retiring and elderly in developed regions; ranked seventh are Western Europe's working age consumers. 141 pages, April 2016.

Made In... Which Country? Perceptions about Brand Origin
http://www.nielsen.com/eu/en/insights/reports/2016/made-in-which-country.html

> Nielsen. On average, 28% of respondents say brand origin is more important than other selection factors such as price and quality, but Europeans are likelier to say brand origin is less important than other factors (35%). 28 pages, April 2016. (Registration required.)

Thinking Big: Eversheds' Practical Guide to International Expansion for Retailers
http://consumerhub.eversheds.com/knowledge-centre/thinking-big-eversheds-practical-guide-to-international-expansion-for-retailers

> Eversheds. Practical steps and issues to consider when expanding your business, from identifying the expansion opportunity through to market launch. 21 pages, Sept. 2016.

Global Connected Commerce
http://www.nielsen.com/ca/en/insights/reports/2016/global-connected-commerce.html

Nielsen. Survey to determine what motivates & deters consumers to make a purchase online. Countries surveyed include France, Germany, Italy, Poland, Spain, Turkey & the UK. 38 pages, Jan. 2016. (Registration required.)

Global E-commerce Report 2017
https://www.ecommercewiki.org/Prot:C_Light_Global_Report_v170920_-_FINAL

Ecommerce Foundation for Global Ecommerce Association. Statistics and trends for the consumer e-commerce market, including France, Germany, Italy, Spain, Turkey and the UK. Separate reports available for Sweden, Denmark and Portugal. 144 pages, 2017. (Registration required.)

Top Markets Series
http://trade.gov/topmarkets

US International Trade Administration. Written for US exporters, the reports rank future export opportunities. The media and entertainment report includes profiles of the market in Germany, Nordic countries and the UK. The recreational transportation report has a market profile of Western Europe. The travel and tourism report has market profiles for Germany and the UK.

Subsectors

Exporting Home Decoration and Home Textiles to Europe
https://www.cbi.eu/market-information/home-decoration-textiles

Netherlands, Centre for the Promotion of Imports. Intended for exporters from developing countries. Gives tips for finding buyers, channels, and most promising export products.

International Trade and Customs Issues for the Luxury and Fashion Industry
http://www.bakermckenzie.com/en/insight/publications/2017 /07/the-global-legal-guide-for-luxury-and-fashion-co__

Baker McKenzie. Chapter 12 in Global Legal Guide for Luxury and Fashion Companies. Covers customs valuation, classification, country-of-origin marking, preferential rules of origin, products made in the US, and international and regional concerns. 30 pages, 2015.

CIRFS – Members
http://www.cirfs.org/Membership/Categories.aspx

European Man-made Fibres Association. CIRFS are producers of man-made fibres, companies supplying the industry with raw materials or services, and national industry associations.

Placing Toys on the EU Market
https://ec.europa.eu/growth/sectors/toys/placing-on-eu-market_en

European Commission. Steps for importers and links to standards, responsible national authorities, factsheets and guides from Toy Industries of Europe (TIE).

Pleasure Boat International Resource Guide
https://2016.export.gov/industry/marine/index.asp

US Commercial Service & National Marine Manufacturers Association. Written for US recreational marine industry manufacturers, provides information on markets for recreational marine craft, parts, and accessories. 25 country briefs, including Austria, Belgium, Croatia, Czech Republic, Denmark, Finland, France, Germany, Italy, Netherlands, Norway, Poland, Spain, Sweden, Turkey and the UK. 117 pages, 2016.

ICOMIA Recreational Boating Industry Statistics
http://www.icomia.com

International Council of Marine Industry Associations. Global data snapshot, detailed national reports on the industry's largest market countries, key product segments, boat export/import data, marine engine statistics and international boat show statistics. ($)

Guide to the EU Recreational Craft Directive
http://www.europeanboatingindustry.eu/appsite

European Boating Industry. Guide to the EU rules on boats, personal watercraft, engines and components. Detailed chapters on the legal framework, essential safety and environmental requirements, conformity assessment procedures for certification and CE-marking, market surveillance and special cases. ($)

Cosmetics and Personal Care Industry Overview
http://www.cosmeticseurope.eu/cosmetics-industry

Cosmetics Europe. Market information, distribution, cosmetics regulations, labelling and advertising, and contacts at national associations in EU countries.

CosIng [cosmetics ingredients]
http://ec.europa.eu/growth/tools-databases/cosing

European Commission. Database for information on
cosmetic ingredients contained in the Cosmetics
Regulation (EC) No. 1223/2009, the Cosmetics Directive
76/768/EEC, the Inventory of Cosmetic Ingredients, and
Opinions of the Scientific Committee for Consumer Safety.
Main page for cosmetics regulation is
https://ec.europa.eu/growth/sectors/cosmetics_en.

Regulations & standards

Product Safety Legislation
*http://ec.europa.eu/consumers/consumers_safety/product_
safety_legislation/index_en.htm*

European Commission. The General Product Safety
Directive (GPSD) provides a generic definition of a safe
product. Products must comply with this definition. Links
to sector-specific legislation and product specific
provisions for certain categories of products.

Summaries of EU Legislation – Product Labelling and Packaging
http://eur-lex.europa.eu/browse/summaries.html (click on
Consumers icon, then Product labelling and packaging)

EC Eur-Lex. Summaries of EU legislation on consumer
product labelling, including geographic indications,
genetically modified organisms and nutrition, packaging,
eco-labels ("green" labels), and textile products.

EU Ecolabel
http://ecolabel.defra.gov.uk

> GOV.UK. A voluntary mark that can be used to show when a product or service has a reduced impact on the environment. Links to the European Commission website to find out if the product qualifies and how to apply, who can apply, and costs involved.

Green Claims Guidance [UK]
https://www.gov.uk/government/publications/green-claims-guidance

> GOV.UK. Guidance on the use of clear, accurate and relevant environmental claims in marketing and advertising. Links to a guide to making a good environmental claim, and a Green Claims Guidance document.

GDPR Compliance Primer
https://www.iabeurope.eu/policy/iab-europes-gdpr-compliance-primer

> IAB Europe. IAB is the Interactive Advertising Bureau. The primer helps companies comply with Europe's new General Data Protection Regulation (GDPR), which takes effect on 25 May 2018, superseding national data protection laws. 10 pages, May 2017.

Companies & organizations

List of Cluster Organizations
https://www.clustercollaboration.eu/cluster-list

European Cluster Collaboration Platform. Under "sectoral industries", choose apparel, footwear, furniture, leather, recreational goods, etc.; or under "technology fields" choose from several headings under other industrial technologies, to find links to clusters such as the Sports & Technology cluster in Eindhoven, Netherlands. Cluster organizations often provide directories of participating companies, universities and other organizations in the sector.

Brands are an important asset in the consumer marketplace; local owners of popular brands will fiercely protect their local market through litigation if necessary. Remember to check resources in **Section 4b** for guidance on avoiding trademark infringement.

Forest products

Guides & markets

Going Global Export Plan
http://www.wmc-cfb.ca (click on Online Tools)

> Wood Manufacturing Council. Online tool to create an export plan. Modules are Supply chain management; Research and marketing; International trade finance; and Culture and trade.

Entering Foreign Markets: An Opportunity for Ontario's Wood Products Industry
https://fpinnovations.ca/products-and-services/market-and-economics/Documents/2012-ontarios-wood-products-industry.pdf

> FP Innovations. A summary of the 2011 survey of Ontario wood products manufacturers, which identifies export barriers and what type of export assistance is required.

Top Markets Series – Building Products & Sustainable Construction
http://trade.gov/topmarkets/building-products.asp

> US International Trade Administration. Written for US exporters, the reports rank future export opportunities. The building products and sustainable construction report ranks markets for HVACR, lighting, plumbing products, wood products, insulation, windows & doors, and glass. Includes a profile of the UK market.

Forest Products Annual Market Review
http://www.unece.org/forests/fpamr.html

UN Economic Commission for Europe and FAO. Statistics on forest products markets including Europe. Chapters cover an overview of markets, economics and policies, policies shaping forest products markets, pallets and wooden packaging, wood raw materials, sawn softwood, sawn hardwood, wood-based panel, paper, paperboard and wood pulp, wood energy, value-added wood products, and housing and construction. 161 pages, Oct. 2016.

UK and EU Trade of Wood Pellets
https://www.gov.uk/government/statistics/energy-trends-september-2015-special-feature-article-uk-and-eu-trade-of-wood-pellets

UK Dept. of Energy & Climate Change. Overview of UK imports and exports of wood pellets from 2008 to 2015, compared to the European Union trade volumes. 6 pages, Sept. 2015.

Regulations & standards

Promoting Sustainable Building Materials
https://www.unece.org/fileadmin/DAM/timber/publications/SP-38.pdf

UN Economic Commission for Europe and FAO. Profiles policies and programs from Austria, Germany, Switzerland, Netherlands and the UK, among others. 124 pages, Sept. 2016.

Companies & organizations

CEPI – Members
http://www.cepi.org/about-us/cepi-members

Confederation of European Paper Industries. Directory of national paper associations in Europe.

ETTF – Members
http://www.ettf.info/members

European Timber Trade Federation. ETTF represents the key importing national timber trade federations in Europe.

List of Cluster Organizations
https://www.clustercollaboration.eu/cluster-list

European Cluster Collaboration Platform. Under "sectoral industries", choose forestry, furniture, wood products, etc., to find links to clusters such as the Estonian Wooden Houses Cluster in Tallinn. Cluster organizations often provide directories of participating companies, universities and other organizations in the sector.

Support for market research & market entry

Wood Exports
https://www.ontario.ca/page/wood-exports

Ontario Ministry of Natural Resources and Forestry. The ministry provides advice and market information to exporters and supports studies to help the industry expand or recover market share in its traditional European market.

Canada Wood
http://canadawood.org

Canada Wood Group. Helps wood products manufacturers expand in overseas markets including Europe. Two programs – Market access: guidance on product standards and phytosanitary issues and Market development: missions, trade fairs, demonstration projects, etc.

FedNor – Innovation Fund
http://fednor.gc.ca/eic/site/fednor-fednor.nsf/eng/fn03444.html

FedNor. Eligible project activities include a) activities related to applied R&D with commercial market potential, including early stage marketing, outreach and promotional initiatives, product, process and service certifications, and market research and technical studies to determine needs and direct future R&D and b) activities that enable organizations and SMEs to increase the level of innovation, productivity, quality and competitiveness in key sectors, including forest industries.

Information and communications technologies

Guides & markets

Top Markets Series
http://trade.gov/topmarkets

US International Trade Administration. Written for US exporters, the reports rank future export opportunities within 27 industries including cloud computing, financial technology, health IT, and smart grid. Each industry report provides a market assessment of the competitiveness, opportunities and challenges within a sector. Case studies for cloud computing in Germany & the UK, financial technology in the UK, health IT in Denmark, Germany & Turkey, and smart grid in Turkey & the UK.

Digital Transformation Scoreboard 2017
http://ec.europa.eu/DocsRoom/documents/21501

European Commission. Survey of automotive, mechanical engineering, and healthcare & pharmaceuticals companies on use of social media, mobile service, cloud technologies, internet of things, cybersecurity solutions, robotic & automated machinery, and big data & data analytics. Includes a 2-page profile for each country in EU. 122 pages, Feb. 2017.

Services Profile – Telecommunications
https://www.wto.org/english/res_e/publications_e/serv_profiles 14_e.htm

World Trade Organization. Standard information on key Infrastructure services for 140 economies. For the service sectors including telecommunications, there are about 100 indicators relating to investment, market performance, production, employment, and trade.

ICT Market Reports
https://www.eito.com/countryreports

European IT Observatory. Each country report covers detailed data for 50 market segments, market data and forecasts, analysis of ICT market developments, and an Excel file including the market data. Each report is about 20 pages. ($)

European Semiconductor Statistics
http://www.eusemiconductors.eu/esia/industry-statistics/semiconductor-market

European Semiconductor Industry Association. ESIA is a licensee of WSTS (World Semiconductor Trade Statistics) data for Europe, the Middle East and Africa; it publishes brief monthly statistics reports for Europe. ($)

Information Economy
http://unctadstat.unctad.org/wds/ReportFolders/reportFolders.aspx

UN Conference on Trade & Development. Expand the "information economy" folder to find statistics tables for ICT goods percentage share of total trade, bilateral trade flows by ICT goods category, and core indicators on ICT use in business.

Regulations & standards

Export Permits for Cryptographic Items
http://www.international.gc.ca/controls-controles/export-exportation/crypto/Crypto_Intro.aspx

Global Affairs Canada. Explains export permit applications for information security goods/technology and goods/technology employing cryptography.

ICT-Eye
http://www.itu.int/net4/itu-d/icteye

UN International Telecommunication Union. A portal for telecommunication/ICT indicators and statistics, regulatory and policy information, national tariff policies and costing practices. Covers broadband, internet, mobile, VoIP, fixed-wired, and spectrum regulation. Includes 2- to 3-page guides for 43 countries in Europe, from Albania to Vatican.

Services Trade Restrictiveness Index
http://www.oecd.org/tad/services-trade/services-trade-restrictiveness-index.htm

OECD. The Index helps identify which policy measures restrict trade. Country notes offer a 2-page analytical summary of services trade restrictiveness in each of 44 countries, mainly in Europe. Sector Notes provide an analysis of the 18 different services sectors including computers, telecommunications, and television & broadcasting. The Regulatory Database covers specific laws and regulations that contribute to services trade restrictiveness – filter by sector and country.

Companies & organizations

Deloitte Technology Fast 50 Central Europe
https://www2.deloitte.com/cefast50

Deloitte. Brief profiles of fast-growing companies in sectors including IT & digital solutions and media & telecommunications. Companies are headquartered in Bosnia & Herzegovina, Bulgaria, Croatia, the Czech Republic, Hungary, Lithuania, Poland, Romania, Serbia, Slovakia or Slovenia. 68 pages, 2016.

Electronic Services Directory

https://www.ventureoutsource.com/contract-manufacturing/search-ems-resources-directory

> VentureOutsource.com. Directory of electronics products and services; search by facilities location, services offered, or target sector.

List of Cluster Organizations

https://www.clustercollaboration.eu/cluster-list

> European Cluster Collaboration Platform. Under "emerging industries", choose digital industries or mobility technologies; under "technology fields" look under electronics, to find links to clusters such as the BrainsBusiness-ICT North Denmark cluster in Aalborg, Denmark. Cluster organizations often provide directories of participating companies, universities and other organizations in the sector.

Support for market research & market entry

ITAC SME Portal

http://itac.ca/smeportal

> Information Technology Association of Canada. Membership organization for Canadian SMEs in information technology. Offers events, learning opportunities, trade missions, business connections through peer networks, and access to funding opportunities.

Early Stage Exporters
http://www.occ.ca/programs/early-stage-exporters

Ontario Chamber of Commerce. Four categories of activities are funded: direct contacts, marketing tools, market research and foreign bidding projects. Companies must be in a priority sector: Advanced manufacturing; Aerospace; Building products and construction; Clean technology; Exportable professional services (e.g., engineering); ICT including digital media; and Life sciences.

FedNor – Innovation Fund
http://fednor.gc.ca/eic/site/fednor-fednor.nsf/eng/fn03444.html

FedNor. Eligible project activities include: a) activities related to applied R&D with commercial market potential, including early stage marketing, outreach and promotional initiatives, product, process and service certifications, and market research and technical studies to determine needs and direct future R&D and b) activities that enable organizations and SMEs to increase the level of innovation, productivity, quality and competitiveness in key sectors, including ICT.

Life sciences

Guides & markets

Healthcare Technologies Resource Guide
http://2016.export.gov/industry/health/healthcareresourceguide
/eg_main_083726.asp

US Commercial Service. Written for US exporters, the guide offers market briefs on 70 countries, including 23 European countries from Austria to the UK. Each country analysis covers market entry and current market trends, such as current demand and barriers to entry. Subsector matrix ranks export potential matrix for specific sub-sector exports in each country. 303 pages, 2017.

Top Markets Series
http://trade.gov/topmarkets

US International Trade Administration. Written for US exporters, the reports rank future export opportunities within 27 industries including health IT, medical devices, and pharmaceuticals. Each industry report provides a market assessment of the competitiveness, opportunities and challenges within a sector. Case studies include health IT in Denmark, Germany &Turkey, medical devices in Germany, and pharmaceuticals in Turkey.

2015 Global Health Care Sector Outlook
http://www2.deloitte.com/be/en/pages/life-sciences-and-
healthcare/articles/global-health-care-sector-outlook.html

Deloitte. Covers current issues impacting the global healthcare sector, and provides a snapshot of activity in a number of geographic markets, including Germany and the UK.

Global Health's New Entrants
https://www.pwc.com/gx/en/industries/healthcare/publications/
new-entrants.html

> PwC. New entrants from outside the traditional business of healthcare are redefining the healthcare market, bringing innovative business models, more affordable and convenient care options, wellness and fitness, and more, to address longstanding challenges. 24 pages, March 2015.

The Pharmaceutical Industry in Figures
https://www.efpia.eu/media/219735/efpia-
pharmafigures2017_statisticbroch_v04-final.pdf

> European Federation of Pharmaceutical Industries & Associations. Industry statistics, R&D expenditure by country, industry production and employment by country, retail price components, VAT by country, generics, and imports by country. 28 pages, 2017.

Regulations & standards

An Introduction to Medical Device Legislation in the European Union
https://www.export.gov/article?id=An-Introduction-to-
Medical-Device-Legislation-in-the-European-Union

> US Dept. of Commerce. Covers legislation, CE marking, compliance with requirements, modules of conformity, authorized representatives and other issues. Feb. 2017.

Exporting Medical and Laboratory Devices to Europe
https://www.cbi.eu/market-information/medical-laboratory-devices

Netherlands, Centre for the Promotion of Imports. Intended for exporters from developing countries; gives tips for finding buyers, channels, and most promising export products.

Medical Devices Global Practice Guide
http://www.lexmundi.com/lexmundi/Medical_Devices_Guide.asp

Lex Mundi. Overview of the medical device regulations in Austria, Cyprus, Czech Republic, Estonia, Finland, Ireland, Latvia, Lithuania, Poland, Romania, Switzerland, and Ukraine. 140 pages, 2012.

Companies & organizations

Medtech Europe – National Associations
http://www.medtecheurope.org/national-associations

Medtech Europe. Links to the pan-European associations and national associations in 24 countries.

List of Cluster Organizations
https://www.clustercollaboration.eu/cluster-list

European Cluster Collaboration Platform. Under "emerging industries", choose biopharmaceuticals or medical devices; or under "technology fields" look under biological sciences, to find links to clusters such as the ASTER Life Sciences Platform in Bologna, Italy. Cluster organizations often provide directories of participating companies, laboratories, universities and other organizations in the sector.

Support for market research & market entry

Early Stage Exporters
http://www.occ.ca/programs/early-stage-exporters

Ontario Chamber of Commerce. Four categories of activities are funded: direct contacts, marketing tools, market research and foreign bidding projects. Companies must be in a priority sector: Advanced manufacturing; Aerospace; Building products and construction; Clean technology; Exportable professional services; ICT; and Life sciences.

FedNor – Innovation Fund
http://fednor.gc.ca/eic/site/fednor-fednor.nsf/eng/fn03444.html

FedNor. Eligible project activities include a) activities related to applied R&D with commercial market potential, including early stage marketing, outreach and promotional initiatives, product, process and service certifications, and market research and technical studies to determine needs and direct future R&D and b) activities that enable organizations and SMEs to increase the level of innovation, productivity, quality and competitiveness in key sectors, including biotechnology.

Mining, metals & minerals

Guides & markets

European Minerals Yearbook
http://minerals4eu.brgm-rec.fr (click on Yearbook)

> European Minerals Knowledge Data Platform. Data for primary minerals production, trade, resources and reserves. Search by country and commodity. Search for secondary materials by category: mineral-based waste generation, treatment and trade.

Companies & organizations

SupplyMine
http://www.infomine.com/suppliers

> InfoMine, Inc. Database of 20,000 companies covering the entire range of products and services used by the mining industry; filter for European suppliers. Also search for business opportunities. (Registration required.)

EuroMines – Members
http://www.euromines.org/who-we-are/members

> European Association of Mining Industries, Metal Ores & Industrial Minerals. Directory of member associations.

IMA-Europe – Memberships
http://www.ima-europe.eu/about-ima-europe/associations

> Industrial Minerals Association. Click on individual member associations to find membership lists of companies in calcium carbonate, borates, specialty minerals, bentonite, lime, feldspar, silica, talc, diatomite and kaolin.

List of Cluster Organizations
https://www.clustercollaboration.eu/cluster-list

European Cluster Collaboration Platform. Under "sectoral industries", choose metal mining, non-metal mining; or under "technology fields" choose mining technologies, to link to clusters such as the Associação Cluster Portugal Mineral Resources in Estremoz, Portugal. Cluster organizations often have directories of participating companies, universities and other organizations.

Support for market research & market entry

Mining Supply and Services Export Marketing Assistance Program
http://investnorthernontario.com/index.aspx?l=0,1,6,269

Ontario Ministry of Northern Development & Mines and FedNor. Companies engaged in the Strategic "One-on-One" Export Marketing Program can access export marketing financial assistance for trade shows, outbound sales missions, display booths and website development.

FedNor – Innovation Fund
http://fednor.gc.ca/eic/site/fednor-fednor.nsf/eng/fn03444.html

FedNor. Eligible project activities include a) activities related to applied R&D with commercial market potential, including early stage marketing, outreach and promotional initiatives, product, process and service certifications, and market research and technical studies to determine needs and direct future R&D and b) activities that enable organizations and SMEs to increase the level of innovation, productivity, quality and competitiveness in key sectors, including mining.

Professional services

Guides & markets

Services Trade for Principal Partners (2011–2015)
http://www.international.gc.ca/economist-
economiste/statistics-statistiques/principal_partners-
principaux_partenaires.aspx?lang=eng

Global Affairs Canada. Annual data on service exports and imports between Canada and its principal partners. Published in July.

Regulations & standards

Points of Single Contact
http://ec.europa.eu/internal_market/eu-go/index_en.htm

European Commission. The Points of Single Contact (PSCs) are e-government portals for entrepreneurs active in the **service sector**. Find the rules, regulations and formalities that apply to service activities, and administrative procedures, such as "What do I need to do when I want to offer my services abroad on a temporary basis?"

Regulated Professions Database
http://ec.europa.eu/growth/tools-databases/regprof

European Commission. In every EU country, a number of professions are regulated, e.g., pharmacists and architects. The EC provides an online database on professional access requirements across the EU.

Administrative Formalities and Costs Involved in Accessing Markets Cross-Border for Provision of Accountancy, Engineering and Architecture Services
http://publications.europa.eu/en/publication-detail/-/publication/5c8a6c62-44e3-11e7-aea8-01aa75ed71a1

> European Commission. Separate sections for accountancy, engineering and architecture describe types of procedures, regulatory requirements, deadlines, and fees. 217 pages, May 2017.

Services Trade Restrictiveness Index
http://www.oecd.org/tad/services-trade/services-trade-restrictiveness-index.htm

> OECD. The Index helps identify which policy measures restrict trade. Country notes offer a 2-page analytical summary of services trade restrictiveness in each of 44 countries, mainly in Europe. Sector Notes provide an analysis of the 18 different services sectors including accounting, commercial banking, insurance, and legal. The Regulatory Database covers specific laws and regulations that contribute to services trade restrictiveness – filter by sector and country.

Companies & organizations

Trade Services Directory
http://www.globaltrade.net/expert-service-provider.html

> GlobalTrade.net. Directory of trade service providers worldwide, including banks, language services, lawyers, taxes, trade compliance and customs, trading companies and agents. Search by service category, country or keyword.

List of Cluster Organizations
https://www.clustercollaboration.eu/cluster-list

European Cluster Collaboration Platform. Under "sectoral industries", choose business services, financial services, insurance services, printing services; or under "emerging industries" choose experience industries or logistical services, to find links to clusters such as the Smart Cities Mediterranean Cluster in Limassol, Cyprus. Cluster organizations often provide directories of participating companies, universities and other organizations in the sector.

Support for market research & market entry

Early Stage Exporters
http://www.occ.ca/programs/early-stage-exporters

Ontario Chamber of Commerce. Four categories of activities are funded: direct contacts, marketing tools, market research and foreign bidding projects. Companies must be in a priority sector: Advanced manufacturing; Aerospace; Building products and construction; Clean technology (including renewable energy and environmental technologies); Exportable professional services (e.g. architecture, engineering, urban planning); ICT including digital media; or Life sciences.

Public sector procurement

Guides

European Union Government Procurement Guide for Canadian Businesses
http://www.international.gc.ca/gac-amc/assets/pdfs/publications/European-Union-Government-Procurement-Guide-ENG.pdf

> Global Affairs Canada. The Guide has these aims: Increase awareness of government-procurement laws, regulations and procedures applicable in the EU; Foster compliance with EU requirements; and Promote the effective and consistent use of information sources and EU-tendering practices across Canada. Chapters include Overview of the EU process; CETA government procurement commitments; Challenges and expectations for bidders; Guide to using TED; Completing a bid; Selection and award criteria; procurement procedures; Thresholds; Remedies; and Background information. 50 pages, 2017.

International Project Bids
http://publications.gc.ca/site/eng/9.686807/publication.html

> Team Canada Inc. Useful advice on researching the country and project, evaluation criteria and negotiation with potential partners, and proposal development and analysis. (Note: Contacts and links for identifying potential projects are now out-of-date.) 13 pages, 2003.

Buying green! A handbook on green public procurement
*http:// publications.europa.eu/en/publication-detail/-
/publication/8c2da441-f63c-11e5-8529-01aa75ed71a1*

European Commission. Written for public authorities
planning green public procurement, the handbook follows
the structure of a procurement procedure and gives real
examples of green purchasing by public authorities across
the EU. It should help suppliers and service providers,
particularly SMEs, to understand the environmental
requirements encountered in public tenders. 80 pages,
2016.

Public Procurement Guide
http://www.lexmundi.com/lexmundi/Public_Procurement_Guide2.asp

Lex Mundi. Overview of the legal framework for
government procurement. Countries covered include
Austria, Belgium, Bulgaria, France, Greece, Latvia,
Poland, Portugal, Serbia, Switzerland and Turkey. 187
pages, Oct. 2012.

**Selling to United Nations Agencies: A Guide for Canadian
Businesses**
*http://tradecommissioner.gc.ca/development-
developpement/143253.aspx?lang=eng*

Trade Commissioner Service. Identifying opportunities
with UN agencies; Registering as a vendor; Marketing to
UN agencies; Procurement documents and competitions;
and Bidding, evaluation and contract execution. Feb. 2016.

Business Opportunities: Development and Humanitarian Aid Markets
http:// tradecommissioner.gc.ca/eng/development-humanitarian-aid-markets/index.jsp

> Trade Commissioner Service. Explanation of markets in developing countries and humanitarian relief. Links to development banks, aid agencies, and a Partnering Guide *http://tradecommissioner.gc.ca/development-developpement/mdb-partnering-guide-guide-partenariat-bmd.aspx* which covers how to find a partner, types of relationships, mitigating risks and tips.

e-GPA Portal
https://e-gpa.wto.org

> World Trade Organization – Government Procurement Agreement. Portal to market access information about signatories, currently including Canada, EU, Iceland, Liechtenstein, Montenegro, Norway, Switzerland, Ukraine and the US. Indicates which government agencies and which products, services and construction services are included, and the threshold values above which individual procurements are subject to the GPA disciplines.

Find opportunities

TED – Tenders Electronic Daily
http://ted.europa.eu/TED/main/HomePage.do (choose language)

> TED provides free access to business opportunities from the European Union, the European Economic Area and beyond. Every day from Tuesday to Saturday, about 1700 public procurement notices are published – 460,000 calls for tenders per year, for about €420 billion of value. Browse, search and sort procurement notices by country, region, business sector and more.

Contracts Finder [UK]
https://www.gov.uk/tendering-for-public-sector-contracts/overview

UK Government. Search for information on contracts worth over £10,000 with the government and its agencies. Search for contract opportunities by sector and for details of previous tenders and contracts. **Scotland, Wales and Northern Ireland** have their own websites: Public Contracts Scotland *http://www.gov.scot/Topics/Government/Procurement*; Sell2Wales *https://www.sell2wales.gov.wales*; and eSourcing NI *https://e-sourcingni.bravosolution.co.uk/web/login.shtml*.

La PLACE – Plate-forme des Achats de l'État
https://www.marches-publics.gouv.fr

République Française. Purchasing platform for départements and chambers of commerce. Quick search by département. The site offers user guides and a practice area in the Help section of the website.

BOAMP.fr
http://www.boamp.fr

Bulletin officiel des annonces des marchés publics. French contracts above €90,000, but below the TED threshold, are advertised on BOAMP. BOAMP also provides practical advice on replying to tenders.

United Nations Global Marketplace
https://www.ungm.org

The United Nations represents a global market of over USD 17 billion annually for all types of products and services. The UNGM acts as a single window through which potential suppliers may register with the UN organizations using the UNGM as their vendor database. The UNGM provides an excellent springboard to introduce your products and services to many UN organizations, countries and regions by completing only one registration form.

Support for market entry

Canadian Commercial Corporation
http://www.ccc.ca

Helps Canadian exporters access foreign government procurement markets through government to government contracting; it has negotiated Memoranda of Understanding with various foreign government buyers for acquisitions from Canada. Sectors of focus include civil aerospace; construction & infrastructure; cleantech, environment & energy; ICT & security; and defence.

7. Market entry

7a. Trade leads
7b. Trade shows
7c. Distribution channels
7d. e-Commerce
7d. Promotion

You may find business opportunities on trade leads websites – see subsection 7a – or receive unsolicited orders from your website. More likely, you will have to work at meeting potential foreign buyers through trade shows, either independently or with government support – see subsection 7b. Participating in a trade show in the target market is also an opportunity to undertake local primary market research.

Your choice of local market entry partner, such as a distributor or a sales agent, will depend on the buying practices of your sector and of the local market. Guides on making this choice and on contracts, and directories of potential partners, are covered in subsection 7c; see also Section 5 for more general company directories.

Making sure your website is optimized for sales in the target market is a market entry option covered in subsection 7d, which includes resources describing e-Commerce in Europe and programs to help Canadian SMEs with e-commerce in exporting. See also Section 6 Consumer products & services for resources that will help with online retail.

Promotion of your products and services in the target market is a long-term component of your export plan. Subsection 7e includes some resources for planning brand and in-market advertising options.

Sector-specific options for attracting the attention of potential buyers, such as joining industry associations and targeting industry clusters, are covered by the resources in Section 6 Sectors.

7a. Trade leads

eMarket Services
http://www.emarketservices.com

Instituto Español de Comercio Exterior. The official European portal for information on e-marketplaces. Provides a Handbook on E-markets, an eMarket Checklist, and a Directory of Electronic Marketplaces with 840 websites sorted by industry sector. (Registration required.)

Trading Hub: Import and Export Trade Leads from Around the Worlds
http://fita.org/tradehub.html

Federation of International Trade Associations. Links to many international trade lead websites, free or fee-based, and geographic- and industry-specific sites.)

Responding to Unsolicited Orders
http://publications.gc.ca/site/eng/9.687624/publication.html

Government of Canada. Use a template to help you draft the price and terms to ask, prepare a quotation for negotiation, and draw up the terms of contract with the foreign buyer. Covers internal research, market research, landed cost calculation, feasibility test (diagnostic), negotiation, the contract, and order fulfillment. 33 pages.

7b. Trade shows

Calendar of Events
https://www.ontario.ca/tradecalendar/search

Ontario Ministry of International Trade. Information about upcoming trade missions, incoming buyers' missions, and exporter workshops such as doing business in the EU, CE marking, and business opportunities in Europe.

ATA Carnet
http://www.chamber.ca/carnet

Canadian Chamber of Commerce. ATA Carnet is an internationally-recognized customs document for the temporary importation of goods. The carnet is commonly used to bring commercial samples to potential customers or trade fairs and by service companies to travel with their professional equipment.

M+A ExpoOrganizer
http://www.expodatabase.com/aussteller/menue/knowhow

Deutscher Fachverlag. Comprehensive collection of task schedules and checklists for trade show planning, operating and follow-up. The website also includes a searchable directory of trade shows, with good coverage of Europe.

Preparing for Trade Shows
http://www.agr.gc.ca/eng/?id=1410072148325 (under Get tips...)

Agriculture and Agri-Food Canada. A series of brief guides provide tips on how to get the most out of trade show participation: Planning and preparation; Marketing and communications; Boothmanship and follow up; Post-show reports.

Intellectual Property Management at Trade Fairs
https://www.iprhelpdesk.eu/sites/default/files/newsdocuments
/Fact-Sheet-IP-management-trade-fairs.pdf

> EU IPR Helpdesk. Recommendations cover registration; IP protection is territorial; keep intangible assets confidential; and limitations of trade fair organizers. 15 pages, May 2017.

EventsEye
http://www.eventseye.com

> EventsEye.com. Bilingual file of 9000 tradeshows, with good coverage for Europe. Search by name, theme, date or location. "Themes" are 150 broad topics, such as Jewelry or Mining Technologies.

ToFairs.com
http://www.tofairs.com

> Expolink Ltd. Database of tradeshows; browse by industry sector, country or region, or search by tradeshow name. Good coverage of Eastern Europe.

Country Travel Advice and Advisories
https://travel.gc.ca/travelling/advisories

> Government of Canada. Safety and security conditions, health questions and entry/exit requirements for the country or countries you may be visiting.

CanExport
http://international.gc.ca/canexport

> Global Affairs Canada. The program supports Canadian SMEs seeking new export opportunities, particularly in high-growth markets; it reimburses up to 50% of eligible expenses for initiatives to develop new markets, including activities such as participating in trade fairs or doing market research.

Export Market Access
http://exportaccess.ca/en/home

Ontario Chamber of Commerce. Grants available include conducting market research for more precise international market targeting, making direct contacts at international trade shows, and preparing for incoming or outgoing missions.

7c. Distribution channels

Finding, Training and Managing International Agents and Distributors
http://www.edc.ca/EN/Knowledge-Centre/Publications (click on Growth)

Export Development Canada. In markets where there may be language barriers and unfamiliar ways of doing business, working through intermediaries such as agents and distributors may be the best approach. This paper covers the issues that exporters should consider if they decide to adopt this strategy: types of intermediaries, finding and qualifying intermediaries, the legal perspective, and motivating international intermediaries. 15 pages, 2016. (Registration required.)

Strategies for Optimizing International Distributors
http://info.ibtpartners.com/finding-distributors-for-export-markets

IBT Partners. Whitepaper covers agents vs. distributors, identifying distributors online and offline, engaging distributors online and offline, supporting your distributors, managing distributor networks and best practice recommendations. (Registration required.)

come-into-contact.com
http://www.iucab.com/en/looking_for_agents.php

Internationally United Commercial Agents and Brokers. Links to the member directories of 14 affiliated associations of commercial agents. Choose first the country/region, then search by industry sector. Coverage includes Austria, the Nordics (i.e. Finland, Norway, Sweden, and Denmark), France, Germany, Italy, Netherlands, southeast Europe (i.e. Cyprus, Greece, and Slovenia), Spain, Switzerland, and the UK.

Trading Companies and Agents
http://www.globaltrade.net/global/Sales-and-Distribution/expert-service-provider.html

GlobalTrade.net. Nearly 8000 distributors, export management companies, trading companies and sales agents. Filter by 15 industry sectors, from chemicals to vehicles/parts.

Commercial Contract Terms
http://www.edc.ca/EN/Knowledge-Centre/Publications/Pages/default.aspx

Export Development Canada. Covers commercial contract principles and typical clauses. (Registration required.)

Model Contracts for Small Firms
http://www.intracen.org/model-contracts-for-small-firms

UN/WTO International Trade Centre. Leading law firms from 51 countries created models that – with minimal modifications – can be used for contracts in any part of the world. The Model Contracts cover key trade activities such as sale of goods, distribution, services, and joint ventures.

Enforcing Contracts – Bulgaria, Hungary and Romania
http://www.doingbusiness.org/data/exploretopics/enforcing-contracts/eu-bulgaria-hungary-romania

World Bank. For 22 cities, compares the time, cost and number of procedures in a sale of goods dispute. July 2017.

Enforcing Contracts – Poland
http://www.doingbusiness.org/data/exploretopics/enforcing-contracts/poland

World Bank. For 18 cities, compares the time, cost and number of procedures in a sale of goods dispute. June 2015.

7d. e-Commerce

E-Commerce Figures per Country
https://www.ecommerce-europe.eu/research/figures-per-country

Ecommerce Europe. Summaries of e-commerce statistics by country, such as average spending per online shopper, percentage of total turnover sales on e-commerce, and VAT-rate. Ecommerce Europe represents over 25,000 online stores across Europe; click on About Us to link to 20 national associations.

Guide to Global eCommerce
https://www.export.gov/Export-Guides

US International Trade Administration. Cross-border e-commerce articles written for US online retailers. Statistics, trends, B2B and B2C insights, consumer services, regulations, and IP and legal considerations for countries including Belgium, France, Germany, Luxembourg, Netherlands, the Nordic region and the UK. May 2017.

PayPal Cross-Border Consumer Research 2016
*https://www.paypalobjects.com/digitalassets/c/website/marketing/
global/shared/global/media-resources/documents/passport-
citation.pdf*

PayPal with Ipsos. How and why consumers shop online across borders; How consumers pay for cross-border transactions. For example, Portugal is the top country where cross-border online shopping is prevalent; Poland is among the lowest; European buyers lag on adoption of mobile for cross-border purchases. 22 pages, Oct. 2016.

The G20 e-Trade Readiness Index
*https://www.ebaymainstreet.com/policy-papers/g20-e-trade-
readiness-index*

Economist Intelligence Unit for eBay Inc. Ranking of countries on the degree to which they encourage cross-border trade using the Internet. The UK, Germany and France rank in top 10. 20 pages, 2014.

Online Trade, Offline Rules – A Review of Barriers to E-commerce in the EU
*http://www.kommers.se/In-English/Publications/2015/Online-
Trade-Offline-Rules*

Kommersekollegium, National Board of Trade of Sweden. Much of the legal framework for e-commerce, from labelling requirements to the national VAT regimes, is still fragmented within the EU single market. This report lists national and EU rules that restrict online trade, grouped by type (types of product, payment requirements, e-government, ownership of online content, and data protection). 72 pages, 2015.

e-Exporting
https://www.ontario.ca/document/e-exporting

Ontario Ministry of Economic Development & Growth.
Outlines the steps: evaluate your e-export potential,
develop an e-export plan, modify your product for foreign
markets, research the legal issues related to e-exporting,
leverage your website to sell abroad, ship your products,
and get paid; and notes on risks and exporting mistakes.

Succeed with E-commerce
*https://www.bdc.ca/EN/articles-tools/entrepreneur-
toolkit/ebooks/Pages/e-commerce-guide.aspx*

Business Development Bank of Canada. Covers the basics,
from getting your company ready for e-commerce to
launching your online store, and more advanced tips on
how to scale up a basic site to a more sophisticated
presence. It also discusses how to handle the back-end of
e-commerce, including inventory management, order
fulfillment and shipping. (Registration required.)

Voucher for E-Business & Technology Adoption
*http://www.oce-ontario.org/programs/industry-academic-
collaboration/collaboration-voucher-program/VEBTA*

Ontario Centres of Excellence. Connects companies with
expertise at Ontario colleges to help businesses take
advantage of online tools and other technologies for
driving market expansion, including exports. E-business
solutions may include website development, online sales
process, digital and social media, and customer
relationship management.

7e. Promotion

Intellectual Property for Exporting Businesses
http://www.cipo.ic.gc.ca/eic/site/cipointernet-
internetopic.nsf/eng/wr03073.html

>   Canadian Intellectual Property Office. A guide to protecting
>   your intellectual property, including trademarks.

Mondo Times
http://www.mondotimes.com

>   Mondo Code LLC. Database of 33,000 newspapers and
>   trade journals worldwide. Click on "local media by
>   country" to search for local newspapers. Under on the
>   "Magazines" tab, click on "see all topics" to find trade
>   journals. Search by region or country.

ABYZ News Links
http://www.abyznewslinks.com

>   ABYZ Web Links Inc. Newspapers, broadcast, Internet,
>   magazines and press agencies (BU indicates business
>   focus). Search by country; sites include locally-published
>   national and regional sources.

Marketing and Sales Services
http://www.globaltrade.net/global/Marketing-and-
Communications/expert-service-provider.html

>   GlobalTrade.net. International directory includes 8000
>   marketing and sales services. Filter by service type:
>   advertising, B2B marketing, business development,
>   business intelligence, direct marketing, directories and
>   marketplaces, event/tradeshow services,
>   government/NGO procurement services, international
>   trade consulting, market entry, market research,
>   marketing consulting, media/graphic design, packaging

and labelling, public relations, trade data and web marketing services.

SourcefromOntario.com
http://www.sourcefromontario.com

Ontario Investment and Trade Centre. Database to promote Ontario-based suppliers internationally. Search by Ontario industry, company name, product or service.

The Canada Brand
http://www.brandcanada.agr.gc.ca

Agriculture and Agri-Food Canada. A strategy to gain recognition for Canadian food and agriculture products in key markets, helping to differentiate Canadian agriculture and food products from the competition. A suite of tools to help Canadian companies and associations – graphics, promotional material and templates, a photo library, and market research.

Canadian Arctic Capabilities by Sector – Canada
http://international.gc.ca/gac-amc/institution/tcs-sdc/publications/cacg-gcac/cacg-gcac.aspx?lang=eng

Canadian International Arctic Centre, Oslo. Covers ice and ocean technologies and services; clean technologies; cold climate manufacturing; infrastructure, engineering and design; transportation and logistics; mining equipment and services; harsh climate ICT; Arctic aerospace and defence; Northern cultural, creative and specialty food industries.

Canada Wood
http://canadawood.org

> Canada Wood Group. Promotes the environmental reputation of Canada's sustainable forest management practices and increases product knowledge of builders and architects in international markets through seminars, wood demonstration projects and technical literature.

Canadian Construction Materials Centre
http://www.nrc-cnrc.gc.ca/eng/solutions/advisory/ccmc_index.html

> National Research Council of Canada. The Centre works with its counterparts in other countries to identify appropriate assessment requirements and determine the most effective means of obtaining acceptance of Canadian construction-related products.

8. Customs and logistics

8a. Customs
8b. Logistics

While customs issues would not normally be a section in your export plan, the resources in subsection 8a will help you identify the right product classifications for finding the tariffs (customs duties) payable on your products, which in turn will affect the cost of your goods in the destination market. Websites of the local customs agencies may also provide guidance on the correct classification, statement of origin, and local import regulations.

Customs and logistics are important topics at the culmination of your export venture – your logistics team is essential to the physical movement of your products to their destination. Subsection 8b describes resources that will help you understand the contracts and terms of your logistics service providers.

8a. Customs

HS Codes – Keyword Search
http://www.ic.gc.ca/tdo (click on Search By Product)

> Innovation, Science & Economic Development Canada. In the **Trade Data Online** database (TDO), use the Product Search pull-down menu to "search for a product", then enter a keyword to identify HS codes to 6 digits. TDO provides commodity trade data between Canada and its international trading partners, by product or by country, at the 6-digit HS level.

Online Harmonized Commodities Code Database
http://www.asycuda.org/onlinehs.asp

UN Conference on Trade and Development. An official description of the codes in the Harmonized System at the 6-digit level. Browse by code chapters or search by keyword. Currently displays 2012 edition; 2017 edition is in force.

Harmonized System Nomenclature
http://www.wcoomd.org/en/topics/nomenclature/instrument-and-tools.aspx (click on current edition)

World Customs Organization. Browse the hierarchical goods classification system (HS) by chapter. The 2017 edition includes more than 5300 six-digit subheadings.

Canadian Export Classification
http://www.statcan.gc.ca/pub/65-209-x/65-209-x2015000-eng.htm

Statistics Canada. Canadian exporters or their agents must assign an Export HS Number on all export transactions. This manual lists all the possible Export HS Numbers and their accompanying description.

Webinar: Essentials of Exporting
http://www.ciffa.com/education/?Course=essentials-of-exporting&CourseID=2335

Canadian International Freight Forwarders Association. This interactive workshop highlights and clarifies the regulations governing exports from Canada, export reporting procedures, documents and data requirements and timing, and compliance requirements. Provides real-time, instructor-led interaction with questions answered immediately.

Canada Tariff Finder
https://www.tariffinder.ca

BDC, EDC and Global Affairs Canada. Check the tariffs applicable to a specific good of Canadian origin in a foreign market. Currently provides tariff information for 34 countries: United States and Mexico (NAFTA), the 28 EU member states (CETA), Korea (CKFTA), Peru (CPFTA), and Iceland and Switzerland (CEFTA). Search for products by keyword(s) or Harmonized System (HS) code(s). From the standardized 6-digit level displayed, select the most specific tariff level to see tariffs now, and for future years according to the agreed-upon FTA schedule.

Tariff Information by Country
http://www.international.gc.ca/trade-commerce/tariff-tarifaire/index.aspx?lang=eng

Global Affairs Canada. Links to foreign customs tariff databases, by country. The EU's Common Customs Tariff, see **TARIC** below, applies to EU, and Canada has trade agreements with other European countries, such as Iceland and Norway, for which see **Canada Tariff Finder**, above.

EU Online Customs Tariff Database (TARIC)
https://ec.europa.eu/taxation_customs/business/calculation-customs-duties_en (click on TARIC)

European Commission, Taxation and Customs Union. TARIC is a multilingual database that integrates all measures relating to tariff, commercial and agricultural legislation. The search function shows the duty rate and links to any regulations that might apply.

Database: Binding Tariff Information
http://ec.europa.eu/taxation_customs/dds2/ebti/ebti_consultation
.jsp?Lang=en

EC Taxation & Customs Union. A Binding Tariff Information (BTI) decision provides legal certainty of the correct classification in advance. Generally valid for 3 years throughout the EU, regardless of where it is issued, and binding on all EU customs administrations and the holder. The database allows searching for currently valid BTI decisions by keyword.

Tariff Download Facility
http://tariffdata.wto.org

World Trade Organization. Comprehensive database of WTO members' customs tariffs, including European countries not included in the EU Customs Union. The data are the most-favoured nation rates (MFN) and are both the rates actually applied and countries' maximum rates, at the standard 6-digit HS codes.

Tariff Analysis Online
https://tao.wto.org

World Trade Organization. A single interface to two WTO databases: the Integrated Database (IDB) and the Consolidated Tariff Schedules (CTS). Choose a pre-built report such as tariff line duties, principal suppliers, or tariff quotas. Then customize to an import market, year, and one or more 8-digit HS codes. Includes a clear User Guide.

Trade Helpdesk
http://trade.ec.europa.eu/tradehelp

European Commission. Written for developing countries. Sections include requirements & taxes, EU import requirements, VAT rules & excise duties, import tariffs, 10-digit HS codes, trade statistics, and business contacts, including customs and taxation organizations.

National Customs Websites
https://ec.europa.eu/taxation_customs/national-customs-websites_en

EC Taxation and Customs Union. Links to national customs agencies of EU member states and candidate countries.

National Tariff
http://www.wcoomd.org/en/topics/nomenclature/resources/national-and-international-customs-tariff/national-tariff.aspx

World Customs Organization. Links to national customs agencies, including countries not included in the EU Taxation & Customs Union.

8b. Logistics

Incoterms® Rules
https://iccwbo.org/resources-for-business/incoterms-rules

International Chamber of Commerce. Incoterms® are rules that define the responsibilities of sellers and buyers for the delivery of goods under sales contracts and provide a common terminology and descriptions for international shipments. They indicate where the exporter's responsibility ends and the importer's responsibility begins with respect to ownership and insurance of the goods. Summary charts are available from many customs brokers.

ATA Carnet
http://www.chamber.ca/carnet

Canadian Chamber of Commerce. Internationally-recognized customs document for the temporary importation of goods. The carnet is commonly used to bring commercial samples to potential customers or trade fairs and also by service companies to travel with their professional equipment.

UPS TradeAbility
https://wwwapps.ups.com/tradeability?loc=en_CA

UPS. International tools include Harmonizer – identify harmonized tariff codes for your products; Landed cost – estimate the landed cost including applicable duties, fees, taxes, and transportation costs; Denied party screener – search for restricted trading parties or embargoed countries; Import compliance – check for country-specific trade regulations, procedures, tariffs, laws, and administrative rulings; Forms – Complete forms online or browse a library of PDF documents to assist you with export and import shipments. (Registration required.)

CIFFA – Workshops
http://www.ciffa.com/education

Canadian International Freight Forwarders Association.
CIFFA offers web-based training on a regular basis
throughout the year, on topics such as Cargo Insurance,
Incoterms® 2010, Essentials of Exporting, Letters of Credit,
and Understanding the Comprehensive Economic & Trade
Agreement (CETA).

Freight Forwarders and Logistics Directory
http://www.freightnet.com/directory.php

Freightnet. International directory of freight forwarders
and cargo and logistics services, including cargo insurance,
customs brokers, freight associations, couriers, finance
and factoring, shipping lines, track and trace, warehousing
and packaging.

Trade Services Directory
http://www.globaltrade.net/expert-service-provider.html

GlobalTrade.net. Directory of trade service providers
worldwide, including transportation & logistics, trade
compliance and customs, and trading companies and
agents. Search by service category, country or keyword.

Database: Authorised Economic Operators
*http://ec.europa.eu/taxation_customs/dds2/eos/aeo_consultation.
jsp?Lang=en*

EU Taxation & Customs Union. Authorised Economic
Operators/AEOs are certified traders who voluntarily agree
to integrate the AEO program's security and other criteria
into their supply chains, and have agreed to the publication
of their details. AEOs may benefit from simplifications
provided for by the customs rules.

Themes Shaping New Location Selection in Europe
http://www.prologis.com/docs/research/europe/Research_W hitePaper_WhatMattersInEurope_AllEuropeRegions.pdf

> Prologis & EyeForTransport. Warehouse users ranked 100 European locations against 11 criteria. Responses cover key logistics/warehouse location selection criteria, the most desirable locations in Europe today, and key demand drivers of the future. 6 pages, April 2016.

Trading Across Borders
http://www.doingbusiness.org/data/exploretopics/trading-across-borders

> World Bank. Among other measures, the Doing Business database records the time and cost associated with the logistical process of exporting and importing goods, in particular the time and cost (excluding tariffs) associated with three sets of procedures: documentary compliance, border compliance and domestic transport. In 2016, Canada ranks 46th, EU countries rank 1st.

Trading Across Borders in Italy
http://www.doingbusiness.org/data/exploretopics/trading-across-borders-in-italy

> World Bank. Covers the procedural requirements for exporting and importing a standardized cargo of goods. Documents associated with every official procedure are counted – from the contractual agreement between the 2 parties to the delivery of goods – along with the time necessary for completion. Nov. 2012.

Trading Across Borders in Spain
http://www.doingbusiness.org/data/exploretopics/trading-across-borders-in-spain

World Bank. Procedural requirements for exporting and importing a standardized cargo of goods for 5 port cities in Spain. Documents associated with every official procedure are counted – from the contractual agreement between the 2 parties to the delivery of goods – along with the time necessary for completion. Sept. 2015.

Understanding Your Export Costs
https://www.nzte.govt.nz/export-assistance/export-essentials-guides/understanding-your-exporting-costs

New Zealand Trade & Enterprise. Cash flow and sales forecasting and break-even point. 6 pages, April 2017.

Cost to Export (US$ per container)
http://data.worldbank.org/indicator/IC.EXP.COST.CD

World Bank. For each country, gives the fees levied on a 20-foot container in US dollars. All official fees: costs for documents, administrative fees for customs clearance, customs broker fees, terminal handling charges and inland transport, but excluding tariffs and trade taxes. Only official costs are recorded. Several assumptions are made for the business surveyed: size, location, ownership, and level of exporting. Assumes the traded product travels in a dry-cargo, 20-foot, full container load, is not hazardous or subject to export controls, does not require refrigeration, and is not subject to any special phytosanitary or environmental safety standards other than accepted international standards.

After researching the market...

Many of the market research resources described in this toolbox are provided by organizations that are expert in other aspects of international trade. While visiting a website, check out other ways the organization might help you:

Section 2: The Trade Commissioner Service, Ontario Ministry of International Trade and Conference Board of Canada offer workshops and webinars.

Section 3: Export Development Canada provides guidance on financing and insurance for exports.

Section 4: Canadian law, accounting and tax firms have well-connected affiliates in many European countries.

Sections 5 and 6: Chambers of commerce and industry associations often have newsletters alerting members to changing regulations and valuable networking events.

Section 8: BDC's international business development consulting service offers a three-step international growth program: analysis, market selection and market entry strategy. Logistics services also provide market entry support beyond transportation and paperwork.

Next step: Pick up the phone!

9. Bi-lateral associations

9a. In Ontario
9b. In Europe

Bi-lateral associations have members experienced in international trade who may offer advice to new exporters on issues such as market entry and the details of local procedures, and contacts for local service providers in the target market.

9a. Associations in Ontario

European Union Chamber of Commerce in Canada
480 University Avenue, Suite 1500
Toronto, ON M5G 1V2
416-598-7087 *info@euccan.com*
http://www.euccan.com

Canada-**Albania** Business Council
60 Harbour Street, 4th Floor
Toronto, ON M5J 1B7
416-519-9158 *Robert.Baines@atlantic-council.ca*
https://www.canada-albania.com

Belgian Canadian Business Chamber
PO Box 508, 161 Bay Street, 27th Floor
Toronto, ON M5J 2S1
416-816-9154
http://www.belgiumconnect.com

British Canadian Chamber of Trade and Commerce
1411-215 Fort York Blvd.
Toronto, ON M5V 4A2
416-816-9154 *idalia@bcctc.ca*
http://bcctc.ca

Canada **Bulgaria** Business Network
6 Hillholm Road, Unit 1
Toronto, ON M5P 1M2
info@canadabulgaria.com
http://www.canadabulgaria.com

Canadian-**Croatian** Chamber of Commerce
630 The East Mall
Etobicoke, ON M9B 4B1
416-641-2829 *contactus@croat.ca*
http://croat.ca

Cypriot Federation of Canada
6 Thorncliffe Park Drive
Toronto, ON M4H 1H1
416-696-7400 *cypriotfederation@rogers.com*
http://cypriotfederation.ca

Czech Business Association of Canada
205-259 Midpark Way SE
Calgary, AB T2X 1M2
403-264-5150 *cbaconline@gmail.com*
http://www.cbaconline.ca

Canada **Finland** Chamber of Commerce
c/o Finnish Credit Union, 191 Eglinton Ave. East
Toronto, ON M4P 1K1
416-486-1533 *info@canadafinlandcc.com*
http://canadafinlandcc.com

Canadian **German** Chamber of Industry & Commerce
480 University Ave., Suite 1500
Toronto, ON M5G 1V2
416-598-3355 *info.toronto@germanchamber.ca*
http://kanada.ahk.de/en

Hellenic Canadian Board of Trade
PO Box 801, 31 Adelaide St. East,
Toronto, ON M5C 2K1
416-410-4228 *events@hcbt.com*
http://www.hcbt.com

Hungarian-Canadian Chamber of Commerce
PO Box 24 Station Westmount
Montreal, QC H3Z 2T1
514-932-5188 *info@hungariancc.ca*
http://www.hungariancc.ca

Ireland Canada Chamber of Commerce, Toronto Chapter
121 Decarie Circle
Toronto, ON M9B 3J6
cmurphy@icccto.com
http://www.icccto.com

Italian Chamber of Commerce of Ontario
622 College Street, Suite 201 F
Toronto, ON M6G 1B6
416-789-7169 x28 *paina@italchambers.ca*
http://italchambers.ca

Latvia Canada Business Council
4 Credit Union Drive
Toronto, ON M4A 2N8
http://www.latcan.org

Canadian **Netherlands** Business and Professional Association Inc.
PO Box 5073, Station A
Toronto, ON M5W 1N4
info@cnbpa.ca
https://www.cnbpa.ca/

Canada **Poland** Chamber of Commerce of Toronto
2680 Matheson Boulevard E., Suite 102
Mississauga, ON L4W 0A5
info@canada-poland.com
https://canada-poland.com/

Federation of **Portuguese** Canadian Business and Professionals
1136 College Street
Toronto, ON M6H 1B6
416-537-8874 *info@fpcbp.com*
http://www.fpcbp.com

The **Romanian** Business Networking Society
27 Davisbrook Blvd.
Toronto, ON M1T 2H6
http://www.rbn-society.com

Canadian **Serbian** Chamber of Commerce
2520 Dixie Road
Mississauga, ON L4Y 2A5
647-969-8303 *info@canadaserbia.ca*
http://www.canadaserbia.ca

Canadian **Slovenian** Chamber of Commerce
4200 South Service Road
Burlington, ON L7L 4X5
905-632-6400 *info@canslo.com*
http://www.canslo.com

Swedish-Canadian Chamber of Commerce
2 Bloor St. West, Suite 2109
Toronto, ON M4W 3E2
416-925-8661 *info@sccc.ca*
http://sccc.ca

Swiss Canadian Chamber of Commerce (Ontario) Inc.
756 Royal York Rd.
Toronto, ON M8Y 2T6
416-236-0039 *sccc@swissbiz.ca*
http://www.swissbiz.ca

Canada **Turkey** Business Council
60 Harbour Street, 4th Floor
Toronto, ON M5J 1B7
613-806-6728 *general@ctbc.ca*
http://www.ctbc.ca

Turkish Canadian Chamber of Commerce
481 University Ave, Suite 711
Toronto, ON M5G 2E9
416-665-0500 *info@tcccommerce.org*
http://tcccommerce.org

Canada-**Ukraine** Chamber of Commerce
145 Evans Avenue, Suite 211
Toronto, ON M8Z 5X8
416-253-6700 *info@cucc.ca*
http://cucc.ca

9b. Associations in Europe

Eurochambres – Members

> *http://www.eurochambres.eu* (under About Us, click on Our Members)
>
> Association of European Chambers of Commerce and Industry. Click on a printable "contact list", or link to specific member, such as the Federation of Israeli Chambers of Commerce. Many of these local networks have business directories and guides to import.

Chamber of Commerce Canada–**Belgium–Luxembourg**
Avenue Louise 500
1050 Brussels, Belgium
+32 (0) 2 644 90 44 *office@cccbl.org*
http://www.canchambelux.org

Canadian **Bulgarian** Chamber of Commerce
132A Georgi Rakovski Street
First floor, office 3
1000 Sofia, Bulgaria
+359 2 851 72 27 *office@cbcc.org*
http://cbcc.bg

Cyprus-Canada Business Association
38, Grivas Dhigenis Ave.,
PO Box 21455, 1509 Nicosia, Cyprus
+357 22 889 706 *andersson@ccci.org.cy*
www.cypruscanada.com.cy

Canadian Chamber of Commerce in the **Czech Republic**
Národní 1009/3
110 00 Praha 1, Czech Republic
+420 777 400 900 *info@gocanada.cz*
http://www.gocanada.cz

Maggie Weaver | 187

Finnish-Canadian Business Club
c/o Finland Chamber of Commerce
PO Box 1000
00101 Helsinki, Finland
+358 9 4242 6261 *anne.hatanpaa@chamber.fi*
https://kauppayhdistys.fi/finnish-canadian/in-english

Chambre de commerce **France**-Canada
5 rue de Constantine
75007 Paris, France
01 43 59 32 38 *ccfc@ccfc-france-canada.com*
https://ccfc-france-canada.com

German-Canadian Association
Innere Kanalstr. 15
50823 Cologne, Germany
+49 221 2576 781 *info@dkg-online.de*
http://www.dkg-online.de/en

Canadian Chamber of Commerce in **Hungary**
Vármegye u. 3-5
1052 Budapest, Hungary
+36 (30) 827 0199 *info@ccch.hu*
http://ccch.hu

Ireland Canada Business Association
3 Dublin Road
Leixlip, Co. Kildare, Ireland
+ 353 (1) 624 3031 *accounts@irelandcanada.com*
http://www.irelandcanada.com

Italian Chamber of Commerce of Ontario
Via della Moscova, 18
20121 Milano, Italy
+39 (02) 778 8751

Canadian Chamber of Commerce in **Latvia**
Vienības gatve 109
Rīga, Latvia, LV-1058
info@cancham.lv
http://www.cancham.lv

Netherlands-Canada Chamber of Commerce
PO Box 95577
NL 2509CN The Hague, The Netherlands
+31 (70) 2210 555 info@nccc.trade
http://www.nccc.trade

Canadian **Norwegian** Business Association
Box 449, N-1302 Sandvika, Norway
+47 465 48 632 *post@cnba.no*
http://cnba.no

Polish Canadian Chamber of Commerce
ul. Wiejska 17 lok. 13
00-480 Warsaw, Poland
http://pccc.pl

Canadian Council of AmCham **Slovakia**
Hotel Crowne Plaza, 1st floor
Hodžovo námestie 2
811 06 Bratislava, Slovak Republic
+421-2 5464 0534 *office@amcham.sk*
http://www.amcham.sk/canadian-council

Canada-**Spain** Chamber of Commerce
Calle Caracas 15
Madrid, Spain
info@canadaespana.org
http://canadaespana.org/en

Canadian-**Swiss** Chamber of Commerce
Hofackerstrasse 36
8032 Zurich, Switzerland
+41 (0) 79 120 74 29 *info@canswiss.ch*
http://canswiss.ch

Canada-**UK** Chamber of Commerce
Canada House, Trafalgar Square
London SW1Y 5BJ, UK
+44 (0) 207 930 4553
http://www.canada-uk.org

Canada-**Ukraine** Chamber of Commerce
6, Muzeyny Lane, Office 102
Kyiv 01001, Ukraine
+380 (44) 495-8551 *ukraine@cucc.ca*
http://www.cucc.ca

10. Checklist for your export plan

Your export plan is an extension of your business plan, with a focus on international markets. Below is a typical export plan outline, indicating which section of this toolbox will help you research specific parts of your own plan. Some parts of the plan are not helped by market research, such as descriptions of your business or strategic decisions that you have made; for those parts, no sections are indicated.

Export plan elements	Section
Commitment to export ● management commitment ● personnel and export organization ● resources inside the company ● international market goals ● relationship between domestic and export operations ● current strategic alliances ● staffing requirements for exporting	
Products and services ● current products and services ● distinctive features in the target market ● adaptation required for exporting........ ● export control compliance .... ● comparative advantage of production ● future product/service pipeline	 6 4, 6 4a

Market overview	
• political environment	3d
• economic environment	3d
• opportunities	3b, 6, 7a
• industry structure, demand	6
• key market segments	6
• purchase process and buying criteria	
• competitive environment	6
• market share held by imports	3c
• non-tariff barriers	4d
• industry trends & other market factors ...	6
Regulatory & logistical issues	
• intellectual property protection	4b, 6
• other regulatory issues	4a, 6, 8
• transport & insurance	8b
• duties, taxes	8a, 4c
• trade documentation	8
• trade service providers	7c, 8b
Market entry	
• target market(s) & customers	
• key competitors	5,6
• competitive position	
• product positioning	
• pricing strategy	
• contract terms & conditions	7c
• distribution strategy	7c, 7d
• promotion strategy	7b, 7e
• website enhancements	7d
• trade shows	7b
• intermediaries and partners	5, 6, 9b
• sales goals	

Risk factors	
● market risk	3d
● credit and currency risks	3d
● political and other risks	4e
Implementation plan	
● primary target country/customers	
● key activities, marketing efforts	
● evaluation criteria and process	
● secondary targets	
Financial plan	
● revenues	
● operating budget	
● cost of sales	
● marketing & promotion costs	
● other expenses	
Background data	
● on target region/country	2b, 3d
● on target customers	5, 6
List of sources	

Let's look at the export plan sections in a little more detail:

Commitment to export

An export plan is often a prerequisite for participating in a government-sponsored export program. Trade advisors and funding agencies will use it to assess your export readiness. Having an export plan is itself an expression of your commitment; the other elements in this section outline the roles and responsibilities to be assigned and summarize the impact of the export venture on your existing business.

Products and services

Your current line-up of products and services may not all be suitable for export to the target export market, or perhaps not yet.

To be successful in the export market, products and services will need to be distinctive from the local competition and other imports. Study competing products to identify both these distinctive attributes and any adaptations needed to meet local consumer preferences. Other product or service changes may be required to meet regulations and standards. Some products are subject to Canadian export control regulations.

The effort required to make your products competitive in the new market, including the time to adapt production processes, will determine the future product/service pipeline and timing.

Market overview

The elements in this section of the export plan can nearly all be determined through external secondary resources.

Internal sources, i.e. your knowledge of existing customers, will help you decide if an element needs in-depth rather than cursory research. The type of product may determine the importance of a section. For example, for price-sensitive products, economic trends are important; environmental products benefit from changing environmental regulations, regardless of the economy.

Other toolbox sections not noted above may also contribute insights. For example, if opportunities for new business currently arise from your existing clients, you may need to look also in Section 5 Companies to unearth links between your existing customers and potential customers in the export market.

One element in this section, the purchase process and buying criteria, is rarely identified through secondary research. You will probably need a survey of potential buyers or a focus group (i.e. *primary* research) to test how the export customer may differ in that regard from your current customers.

Regulatory & logistical issues

Regulations, standards, and customs documentation are all readily found through secondary research, as are directories of service providers in these areas.

Market entry

In export plans, "target market" most often refers to the region or country that will be the focus of your export planning. In more general plans, target market refers to the key customers or customer segments that will be the focus of your marketing strategy. In either case, the choice of target is yours to make, based not only on your market research, but also on your own experience domestically.

Research on local competitors and current importers should give you insight into the competitive position of your products and services. This insight will help you not only to decide how to position and price your product for success in the market, but will also help you to summarize your decisions on products and timing, in the first section of your export plan.

Sample contracts, for comparison with contracts you have currently with your agents and distributors, can be found through secondary research. The distribution and promotion strategies you choose for the target export market will depend on local market practices and the competition, as well as your own preference.

Participate in trade shows to meet potential buyers, test market acceptance of your product or service, and research competitors. Use the time in-market to also make direct contact with intermediaries and local service providers. From the information gleaned from these in-person meetings, you will be able to establish some sales goals for your exports.

Risk factors

While the risk factors associated with individual countries are well documented in the country guides described in this toolbox, some risks may be specific to your sector or product. The size or complexity of the sale may also bring its own risks, such as participation in infrastructure projects, sales of high-value equipment, or services contracts in the public sector. This section of your export plan is one where Canadian trade advisors expect to find some gaps in your information, and they can help you identify and mitigate those risks.

Implementation plan

The decisions you make based on your market research are summarized in this section of your export plan. Ask your government trade advisor to endorse these expectations.

Financial plan

This section puts numbers to the words of the previous section. It is also a way to monitor the progress of the export venture, and to identify when more or different research needs to be undertaken.

Background data

Secondary market research naturally results in reams of undistilled information. The really pertinent material goes in the appropriate section of the plan as evidence to support your conclusions about your potential success and the decisions you make about implementation. Most of the background information should be just that – in the background. So keep it as an appendix to the plan.

List of resources checked

Last but certainly not least, keep a list of where and when you found the material for each element of the plan. Inevitably you will lose track of which websites were useful and which weren't, and you will make some apparently conflicting notes that you must double-check. When it comes time to update your export plan, this section will be invaluable!

Need help?

Local providers of secondary
market research services can deliver
information from a wide range of resources
to help you estimate a foreign market
and build an export business plan.

Ask these secondary researchers
for ideas on how they can
support your export business:

Clinton Research
gillian@clintonresearch.ca

EDGE Business Information Services
edgebusinfo@gmail.com

FSO Research & Information
info@fsoresearch.ca

Industrious Insights
natalie@industriousinsights.com

Sally Press, Library & Information Services
SPress@rogers.com

Win Global Partners
igor@winglobal.ca